Tokyo Houses

Tokyo Houses

teNeues

Editor in chief: Paco Asensio

Editorial coordination: Haike Falkenberg, Cynthia Reschke

Project coordination and Texts: Nasple & Asakura

Art Director: Mireia Casanovas Soley

Layout: Ignasi Gracia Blanco

Copyediting: Francesc Bombí-Vilaseca, Sabine Würfel

German translation: Inken Wolthaus

French translation: Leïla Marçot

English texts: Nasple & Asakura

English proofreading: Matthew Clarke

Published by teNeues Publishing Group

teNeues Publishing Company
16 West 22nd Street, New York, NY 10010, US
Tel.: 001-212-627-9090, Fax: 001-212-627-9511

teNeues Book Division
Neuer Zollhof 1
40221 Düsseldorf, Germany
Tel.: 0049-(0)211-994597-0, Fax: 0049-(0)211-994597-40

teNeues Publishing UK Ltd.
Aldwych House, 71/91 Aldwych
London WC2B 4HN, UK

www.teneues.com

ISBN: 3-8238-5573-5

Editorial project: © 2002 **LOFT** Publications

Domènech 9, 2-2
08012 Barcelona, Spain
Tel.: 0034 932 183 099
Fax: 0034 932 370 060

e-mail: loft@loftpublications.com
www.loftpublications.com

Printed by: Gràfiques Anman. Sabadell, Spain

August 2002

Die Deutsche Bibliothek – CIP-Einheitsaufnahme
Ein Titeldatensatz für diese Publikation ist bei
der Deutschen Bibliothek erhältlich.

Cover photo: © Katsuhisa Kida
Backcover photo: © Shinkenchiku-Sha

Photos pages: 10, 16, 22 © Naruyasu Nabeshima / e-mai: nabeshima@pop13.odn.ne.jp

Special Thanks to:
Eri Takahashi, Tomoko Ihara, Hiroshi Yamasaki
Kenji & Yoshiko Fujino, Yuko Shimizu and
Nacása & Partners /e-mail: partners@nacasa.co.jp

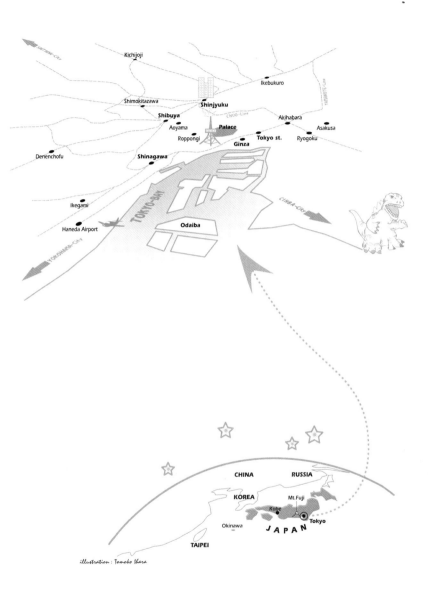

illustration : Tomoko Ihara

Tokyo Map

トウキョウ

・ハウゼス

Tokyo Houses

Originally, the name of Tokyo was Edo. In 1868, with the Meiji revolution that marked the commencement of the the Meiji period, the policy of Japan's self-imposed national isolation which had closed the country to the foreign world was terminated. A process of westernization began. It was at that time that the city of Edo was renamed Tokyo, Eastern Capital, when the emperor's residence was transferred from Kyoto in 1868. It became then the political and imperial capital of Japan, with the inner section of the former Edo castle serving as the new imperial palace.

Nowadays, Tokyo stands at the centre of a vast conurbation that sprawls relentlessly over much of the Kanto region, with a combined population figure of about 27 million. The Tokyo Prefecture itself comprises an area of 2.187 square km containing 23 wards, 27 cities, 1 county , 4 island administrative units and a population of approximately 12 million people.

Despite its many attractions, it could be argued that Tokyo is not a particularly beautiful city. Instead, it is unabashedly confusing, with buildings appearing seemingly overnight. Underlying this chaos is a feeling of impermanence. In Tokyo, everything seems ephemeral. The city was destroyed and rebuilt twice during the last century and is constantly renewing itself.

Since the 50's, and for a period of thirty years Tokyo underwent a stretch of reckless reconstruction, devoid of proper urban planning or of a particular standard building criteria. This was reflected in the policy of the big construction companies' mass-production of prefabricated houses and multistorey apartments, in the usage of artificial, unnatural and cheap materials in their interior design, and in the primary pursuit of economic efficiency only. The above policy was basically known by the "Scrap and Built" phenomenon. Also sudden and constant changes in the landscape of the various Tokyo quarters led to an understandable increase in the use of the word "Mutate", when referring to the perpetual transformation of the city's scenery.

Tokyo is also a city of many attributes and adjectives. The awesome number of automatic vending machines in the streets, the overwhelming presence of convenience stores every 100 metres or so, might not contribute to make it give an appearance of a particularly aesthetic metropolis. Nevertheless, it certainly is a handy and convenient one.

Tokyo boasts a hugely diversified, perfect and impeccable transportation system, comfortable and pleasant offices, department stores and shopping areas brimming over with the best selection of articles from all over the world. It also offers the possibility of sampling the best cuisine from around the globe.

Although for most of the people who have not visited the city, the stereotyped image of an exotic, congested place still prevails, in fact, it must be said that, aside from its various city centers, large areas of this vast city still enjoy an incredibly relaxed atmosphere.

If we were to identify a few of the distinguishing Tokyo lifestyle features that may differ from those of any European city, these could basically be found in the Japanese home. In 90% of Japan's houses, at the entrance, there is a stone step where one takes the shoes off in order to enter the house. A storage closet to put away the shoes is also located in the entrance. Moreover, the use of the futon in the Japanese-style rooms, and a genuine enthusiasm for the bathroom, an exceptional place within the premises, are also distinctive traits.

In this book we try to provide valuable data to enable the reader to peep into the interiors of Tokyo's housing through the works of well known professionals like the celebrated designer Terence Conran, worldwide architects like Cesar Pelli, and highly popular architects and designers like Tezuka Architects, Mikan, Guen Bertheau-Suzuki, Hikone, and Milligram. In it, we also present designers who have studied and successfully adapted the characteristics of traditional Japanese-style architecture into their works like Takatsuka Architecture firm. Other examples are Hijiki House and Watanabe House, portraying a decent, normal and relaxed Tokyo way of life. Finally standard condominiums of privately owned-flats are also presented through the Daikanyama and Itabashi flats.

In this Tokyo Metropolis that invariably goes on rushing at unbelievable speed, amid the vast finished projects on reclaimed land like Odaiba, or the ones that are still taking place along Tokyo Bay, the great majority of Tokyo people are increasingly striving to live in an ecologically friendly environment, at their own pace. Although somewhat late, they are also beginning to rediscover the merits of the old traditions.

The old tendency of Japanese architects to press their own ego translated into an excessively superfluous type of designing which has by now practically become outdated. There is now a growing effort among younger architects to listen more attentively to their clients' personal dreams and to make those come true.

The Japanese traditional architecture had already exerted in the past a remarkable influence among a good number of famous and renown architects like Le Corbusier or Frank Lloyd Wright. Nowadays, many young Japanese architects are seeking to adapt, under different patterns and circumstances, elements of the Japanese traditional architecture into their own design and contemporary lifestyle.

We sincerely hope that this book, aiming at introducing a genuine Tokyo way of life, may also serve as a reference for future urban housing to many people around the world.

Der ursprüngliche Name von Tokio war Edo. 1868 leitete die Meiji-Revolution den Beginn der sogenannten Meiji-Epoche ein, und die Politik der selbst auferlegten nationalen Isolierung, die das Land gegen die Außenwelt abgeschlossen hatte, fand ein Ende. Es begann der Prozess der Verwestlichung. Im Jahre 1868 wurde die kaiserliche Residenz von Kioto nach Edo verlegt und der Name Edo in Tokio umbenannt (die östliche Hauptstadt). Kurz darauf, 1869, wurde Tokio zur politischen und kaiserlichen Hauptstadt Japans. Der innere Teil des früheren Edo-Schlosses wurde zum neuen kaiserlichen Palast umgebaut.

Heute steht Tokio an der Spitze einer riesigen Konurbation mit ca. 27 Millionen Einwohnern, die sich unerbittlich über einen großen Teil der Region von Kanto erstreckt. Darin umfasst die Präfektur von Tokio selbst ein Gebiet von 2187 km, bestehend aus 23 Stadtvierteln, 27 Städten, einer Grafschaft, vier Inseln und einer Einwohnerzahl von ca. 12 Millionen.

Trotz der vielen Attraktionen kann man Tokio nicht gerade als eine schöne Stadt bezeichnen. Im Gegenteil, der Metropole scheint mit ihren neuen Gebäuden, die vermeintlich über Nacht aus dem Boden schießen, ein Zustand permanenten Wandels immanent zu sein, der den Eindruck von Vergänglichkeit vermittelt. In Tokio scheint nichts Bestand zu haben. Diese Stadt, die im vergangenen Jahrhundert zweimal zerstört und wieder aufgebaut wurde, erneuert sich ständig selbst.

Seit den fünfziger Jahren machte Tokio eine Zeit des Wiederaufbaus durch, die in den ersten dreißig Jahren ohne konkrete Stadtplanung und ohne besondere Baukriterien erfolgte. Dies spiegelt sich im Vorgehen der großen Bauunternehmer wider, die ungeheure Mengen an Fertighäusern und vielstöckigen Wohnhäusern unter Verwendung von billigen und künstlichen Materialien für die Inneneinrichtung bauten. Ihr primäres Ziel konzentrierte sich hauptsächlich auf kurzfristigen wirtschaftlichen Gewinn. Diese Politik des Städtebaus wurde später als das Phänomen des „Scrap and Built" bekannt. Die plötzlichen und ständigen Veränderungen des Stadtbildes führten zu der immer häufigeren Verwendung des Ausdruckes „Mutate", wenn man sich auf den beständigen Wandel des Stadtbildes bezog.

Tokio ist eine Stadt mit vielen und mannigfaltigen Attributen und Adjektiven. Die eindrucksvolle Anzahl von Automaten in den Straßen, die erdrückende Menge von rund um die Uhr geöffneten „convenience stores" und allen Arten von Läden, die höchstens 100 Meter voneinander entfernt liegen, tragen zu dem wenig ästhetischen Image der Metropole bei. Diese Charakteristika machen sie jedoch gleichzeitig zu einer leicht zu erobernden Stadt, in der es sich angenehm leben lässt.

Tokio verfügt über ein weit verzweigtes, perfekt funktionierendes öffentliches Transportsystem, über angenehme und bequeme Bürogebäude, große Warenhäuser und Geschäftszentren mit einer unendlichen Auswahl an Produkten aus aller Welt sowie einer breiten Palette von Restaurants mit ausgezeichneter nationaler und internationaler Küche.

Obwohl die meisten Menschen, welche die Stadt nicht besucht haben, sie für einen äußerst exotischen und übervölkerten Ort halten, zeigt die Realität dem Besucher, dass sich ein großer Teil des Lebens in Tokio in einer vollkommen gelassenen und entspannenden Atmosphäre abspielt.

Wenn wir einige der wenigen, im Vergleich zu den westlichen Gepflogenheiten, gegensätzlichen Eigenschaften des Stadtlebens von Tokio definieren müssten, würden wir sie zweifellos im japanischen Heim finden. Beispielsweise verfügen 90% der Häuser im Eingangsbereich über einen Vorraum, in dem sich die Bewohner ihrer Schuhe entledigen. Nach dem Abstellen der Schuhe in einem kleinen Schrank, betritt der Bewohner oder der Besucher den Innenraum des Hauses über eine Stufe, die den Außenbereich von den eigentlichen Wohnräumen trennt. Die Verwendung des Futon in den mit Tatami ausgelegten Zimmern sowie die Hingabe und Sorgfalt, die auf das Badezimmer angewandt werden, gehören ebenfalls zu den Besonderheiten der japanischen Wohnkultur.

Mit diesem Buch möchten wir dem Leser wertvolle Informationen bieten, die es ihm erlauben, einen Blick in das Innenleben der Häuser in Tokio zu werfen. Zu diesem Zweck zeigen wir Arbeiten bekannter Professionals, wie z. B. die Werke des berühmten Designers Terence Conran, von weltberühmten Architekten, wie Cesar Pelli sowie von anderen angesehenen und sehr beliebten Architekten und Designern, wie Tezuka Architects, Mikan, Guen Bertheau-Suzuki, Hikone und milligram. Das Buch beschreibt des weiteren die Projekte von Designern, die in ihre Werke erfolgreich viele Besonderheiten der traditionellen japanischen Architektur integrieren konnten, wie z. B. die Firma Takatsuka Architecture. Beispiele von Projekten wie das Hijiki House und das Watanabe House zeigen uns ein Tokio des gelassenen und entspannenden Lebens, das in vielen Gebieten der Metropole anzutreffen ist. Zum Schluss sind die Apartmenthäuser von Daikanyama und Itabashi zu erwähnen, Vertreter einer anderen Art von Standardwohnungsbau im Tokio von Heute.

Die Bewohner dieser großen und schnelllebigen Metropole mit ihrem Lärm und ihren großen architektonischen Projekten, wie z. B. dem Gebäude von Odaiba oder den noch im Bau begriffenen Gebäuden in der Bucht von Tokio, bemühen sich immer mehr darum, in den Genuss der Vorteile eines Lebens in angenehmer und heller Umgebung zu kommen. Wenn auch ein wenig spät, entdecken sie wieder die Verdienste der alten Traditionen.

Die jungen japanischen Architekten von Heute haben das Ego, das ihre Vorgänger auf ihre Designs übertrugen, geparkt und bemühen sich, in erster Linie die Träume und Wünsche ihrer Kunden zu verwirklichen.

Die traditionelle japanische Architektur hatte bereits spürbar eine Reihe großer Architekten, wie z. B. Le Corbusier oder Frank Lloyd Wright beeinflusst. In der Gegenwart versuchen die jungen japanischen Architekten unter anderen Aspekten und Umständen ihren eigenen Designs und ihrer eigenen Lebensart die Elemente der traditionellen japanischen Architektur anzupassen.

Die Absicht dieses Buches ist es, das wirkliche Tokio anhand von Häusern und Gebäuden in verschiedenen Stadtvierteln der Metropole zu zeigen, und wir würden uns freuen, wenn es auch als Referenz für zukünftige Konstruktionsprojekte in anderen Städten dieses Planeten dienen könnte.

Originellement, Tokyo se nommait Edo. En 1868, avec la révolution Meiji marquant le début de l'ère Meiji, la politique d'isolement national volontaire du Japon qui avait fermé l'accès au pays pour le reste du monde touchait à sa fin. Le processus d'occidentalisation commençait. C'est à cette époque que la cité d'Edo fut rebaptisée Tokyo (Capital de l'Est), lorsque la résidence de l'empereur y fut transférée depuis Kyoto en 1868. Elle devint dès lors la capitale politique et impériale du Japon, la section intérieure de l'ancien château d'Edo accueillant le nouveau palais impérial.

De nos jours, Tokyo se trouve au cœur d'une vaste conurbation qui s'étend inexorablement sur la plupart de la région du Kanto, avec une population globale s'élevant à près de 27 millions de personnes. La Préfecture de Tokyo elle-même couvre une superficie de 2.187 km², comprenant 23 circonscriptions, 1 comté, 4 unités administratives insulaires et une population d'approximativement 12 millions de personnes.

En dépit de ses nombreux attraits, d'aucuns avancent que Tokyo n'est pas une ville particulièrement belle. Qu'elle est plutôt déroutante à l'envi, des immeubles semblant apparaître du jour au lendemain. Sous-tendant ce chaos, un sentiment de provisoire : à Tokyo, tout semble éphémère. La ville a été détruite et reconstruite deux fois au cours du siècle précédent et est en constante rénovation.

Depuis les années 50, et pendant près de trente ans, Tokyo a subi une vague de reconstruction insensée, dépourvue de toute planification urbanistique correcte ou de normes de construction particulières. Les symboles en sont la politique de production massive de maisons préfabriquées et d'appartements en tours par les grandes entreprises de BTP, l'emploi de matériaux artificiels, non naturels et bon marché pour le design intérieur et la poursuite acharnée de la seule rentabilité économique. Cette politique était essentiellement connue comme le phénomène de « Destruction et Construction ». De même, les changements soudains et constants du paysage des divers quartiers de Tokyo engendrèrent un recours sans cesse croissant au terme « Mutation », pour se référer aux transformations perpétuelles du panorama de la cité.

Tokyo est aussi une ville d'épithètes et d'adjectifs. Le nombre stupéfiant de distributeurs automatiques dans les rues ou la présence écrasante de petits bazars tous les 100 mètres ne peuvent contribuer à lui conférer l'apparence d'une métropole particulièrement esthétique. Mais certainement pratique et commode.

Tokyo peut se vanter d'un système de transport diversifié, parfait et irréprochable, de bureaux confortables et plaisants, de grands magasins et de quartiers de shopping débordant des meilleurs produits de l'ensemble du monde. Elle offre également la possibilité de goûter les meilleures cuisines internationales.

Bien que, pour la plupart des personnes qui ne l'ont pas visitée, l'image stéréotypée d'un lieu exotique et congestionné l'emporte encore, il faut préciser, en fait, que loin des divers centres-villes, de vastes zones de la cité bénéficient encore d'une atmosphère incroyablement détendue.

S'il nous fallait identifier quelques-unes unes des caractéristiques du style de vie tokyoïte susceptibles de différer de celui des villes européennes, celles-ci pourraient être découvertes au sein des foyers japonais. Dans 90 % des maisons japonaises, l'entrée présente une marche en pierre permettant à chacun de retirer ses chaussures avant de pénétrer dans la demeure. L'entrée comporte également un placard de rangement pour les entreposer. Plus loin, l'usage du futon dans les chambres de style japonais et un enthousiasme non feint pour les salles de bain, un endroit d'exception parmi les autres pièces, constituent d'autres traits distinctifs.

Avec ce livre, nous allons tenter de proposer quelques clés au lecteur afin de pénétrer les intérieurs des maisons tokyoïtes, en s'appuyant sur les travaux de professionnels reconnus comme le fameux designer Terence Conran, d'architectes internationaux ainsi Cesar Pelli et d'architectes et designers très populaires comme Tezuka Architects, Mikan, Guen Bertheau-Suzuki, Hikone et milligram. Ici, nous présenterons aussi des créateurs ayant étudié et adapté avec succès les caractéristiques de l'architecture japonaise traditionnelle dans leurs œuvres, comme la société Takatsuka Architecture. D'autres exemples en sont les maisons Hijiki et Watanabe, dépeignant un style de vie simple, normal et détendu au cœur de Tokyo. Enfin, des résidences d'appartements privés sont également présentées avec les appartements Daikanyama et Itabashi.

Au cœur de cette métropole qu'est Tokyo, toujours en ébullition, parmi les nombreux projets menés à bien sur des terrains gagnées sur la mer comme à Odaiba, ou ceux en cours le long de la baie de Tokyo, la majeure partie des habitants luttent de plus en plus pour vivre dans un environnement respectueux de la nature, selon leur propre rythme. Bien qu'un peu tard, ils commencent à redécouvrir les mérites des traditions ancestrales.

L'ancienne tendance des architectes japonais, traduisant leur ego dans un genre créatif excessivement superflu, est désormais pratiquement révolue. Un effort croissant d'écoute des rêves personnels des clients et de matérialisation de ces rêves est aujourd'hui notable parmi les jeunes architectes.

L'architecture japonaise traditionnelle avait déjà, par le passé, exercé une influence remarquable sur nombre d'architectes connus et reconnus, ainsi le Corbusier ou Frank Lloyd Wright. De nos jours, beaucoup de jeunes architectes japonais cherchent à adapter, selon diverses formes et circonstances, des éléments de l'architecture traditionnelle pour les intégrer à leur design personnel et à un style de vie contemporain.

Nous espérons sincèrement que ce livre, visant à présenter le style de vie tokyoïte authentique, pourra également servir de référence aux logements urbains de demain pour tous et partout de par le monde.

1. In every Japanese-style room fitted with tatami flooring there is a special closet where to keep the futon called "Oshiire".

2. In general the futon is kept in the "Oshiire" during the daytime. At night it is spread out on the tatami floor. Due to the humidity of the Japanese climate, the futon is also frequently aired in the sun a few hours during the morning time.

3. The special closet "Oshiire" is covered by a sliding door called "Fusuma".

1. In allen japanischen Zimmern, die mit Tatami Teppichen versehen sind, gibt es einen speziellen Schrank namens „Oshiire", um den Futon aufzubewahren.

2. Normalerweise wird der Futon tagsüber im „Oshiire" aufbewahrt und nachts herausgeholt, auf dem Tatami ausgebreitet, um darauf zu schlafen. Wegen des feuchten Klimas in Japan wird das Futon gelegendlich morgens in der Sonne gelüftet.

3. Der Schrank „Oshiire" ist mit einer Schiebetüre namens „Fusuma" versehen.

1. Chaque pièce de style japonais comportant un sol en tatamis est dotée d'un placard spécial où ranger le futon appelé « Oshiire ».

2. En général, le futon reste dans l'« Oshiire » durant la journée. De nuit, il est étendu sur le sol en tatamis. En raison de l'humidité du climat japonais, le futon est également fréquemment aéré au soleil quelques-heures dans la matinée.

3. Le placard spécial, « Oshiire » est fermé par une porte coulissante nommée « Fusuma ».

1. En todas las habitaciones de estilo japonés equipadas con suelo de tatami existe un armario especial denominado *oshiire* para guardar el futon.

2. Generalmente el futon se coloca dentro del *oshiire* durante el día y se saca durante la noche, extendiéndolo sobre el tatami para dormir. La humedad del clima en Japón hace que el futon sea tendido al sol unas horas durante la mañana para que se pueda airearse.

3. El armario *oshiire* está cubierto por una puerta corredera denominada *fusuma*.

Originalmente el nombre de Tokio era Edo. En 1868, comienza un proceso de modernización, también conocido por el término occidentalización, en el que, a partir de la revolución Meiji que tuvo lugar este año y con el consiguiente advenimiento de la era Meiji, se daba por terminado el largo período de autoimpuesto aislamiento que Japón había mantenido frente al resto del mundo. Es en esta misma época que la ciudad de Edo pasa a denominarse Tokio, "Capital del Este", con motivo del traslado a la misma en 1868 de la residencia del emperador desde la ciudad de Kioto. Tokio se convierte entonces en la capital imperial y política del país.

En la actualidad, la ciudad de Tokio preside una inmensa conurbación de unos 27 millones de habitantes que se extiende implacablemente sobre gran parte de la región de Kanto. Dentro de la misma, la prefectura de Tokio por sí sola comprende un área de 2.187 km^2 compuesta por 23 barrios, 27 ciudades, un condado, cuatro islas y una población aproximada de doce millones de personas.

A pesar de sus muchos atractivos, bien podría decirse que Tokio no es una ciudad particularmente bella. Al contrario, la metrópolis parece reivindicar un cierto estado de confusión permanente, con edificios nuevos que aparecen de la noche al día. Una cierta sensación de que nada es duradero ni perenne explica este caos. En Tokio todo parece efímero. La ciudad, destruida y reconstruida dos veces durante el pasado siglo, está siempre renovándose a sí misma.

Desde la década de los cincuenta, y por un periodo de treinta años, Tokio sufrió una etapa de reconstrucción poco juiciosa, carente de un adecuado criterio de planificación urbana. Un reflejo de ello lo encontramos en la forma de funcionar de las grandes constructoras, produciendo cantidades ingentes de casas prefabricadas y apartamentos de pisos, utilizando para su interiorismo materiales baratos y artificiales, y para las cuales, el objetivo primordial se reducía a criterios de rentabilidad económica a corto plazo, sin más. Esta política de construcción se conoció posteriormente como el fenómeno del *Scrap and Build* (desguazar y construir). Asimismo, los bruscos y constantes cambios que se daban en el paisajismo urbano de la ciudad propiciaron también el uso del término *Mutate* para referirse a la constante transformación del decorado urbano.

Tokio es ciudad de muchos y variados atributos y características.

El impresionante número de máquinas expendedoras automáticas en las calles, la abrumadora presencia de colmados para todo tipo de productos, abiertos las 24 horas del día y separados entre sí por no más de cien metros, contribuyen a que esta metrópolis proyecte una imagen poco estética de sí misma. No obstante, son estos mismos rasgos los que hacen que esta sea una ciudad profundamente accesible y cómoda para vivir.

Tokio se precia de poseer por otra parte un amplio, diversificado e impecable sistema de transporte público, agradables y cómodos edificios de oficinas, grandes almacenes y áreas comerciales rebosantes de la mejor selección de productos procedentes de todo el mundo, así como una amplísima gama de restaurantes que permite degustar tanto la riquísima cocina autóctona como todo tipo de cocina internacional.

Aunque la imagen estereotipada dominante, sobretodo para aquellos que no han visitado la ciudad, es la de un lugar eminentemente exótico y repleto de gente, la realidad permite hacer ver al visitante que gran parte de la vida de Tokio se desarrolla en un ambiente totalmente pausado y relajante.

Si tuviéramos que identificar algunas de las pocas características diferenciadoras de la vida urbana de Tokio con respecto a la de Occidente, éstas se encontrarían sin lugar a dudas dentro de la casa japonesa. El 90% de las mismas posee en la entrada un espacio intermedio utilizado por sus moradores para quitarse los zapatos. Una vez colocados éstos en un pequeño armario situado en la misma entrada, el inquilino o visitante a la misma accederá al interior de la casa subiendo el escalón que separa la zona exterior de las dependencias interiores. El uso del futon en el interior de las habitaciones de estilo japonés con tatami, y la pasión y esmero con que se recrea el espacio dedicado al baño son otras de las peculiaridades que presenta la casa japonesa.

Con la edición de este libro pretendemos proporcionar al lector una valiosa información que le permitirá adentrarse en el interior de la vida de las casas de Tokio mediante el trabajo de conocidos profesionales como el célebre diseñador Terence Conran, de arquitectos mundialmente famosos como Cesar Pelli, además de otros arquitectos y diseñadores que gozan de gran prestigio y popularidad como Tezuka Architects, Mikan, Guen Bertheau-Suzuki, Hikone y Milligram. El libro presenta también el trabajo de diseñadores que han estudiado y adaptado con éxito a sus obras muchas de las peculiaridades de la arquitectura tradicional japonesa como Takatsuka Architecture Firm. Ejemplos de obras como Hijiki House y Watanabe House nos muestran este Tokio de vida pausada y relajante existente en muchas áreas de la metrópolis. Los edificios de apartamentos de Daikanyama e Itabashi representan otro tipo de vivienda estándar del Tokio de hoy en día.

Los habitantes de esta gran metrópolis que vive apresuradamente en medio del bullicio de sus grandes proyectos arquitectónicos como el de Odaiba u otros aún en curso en la bahía de Tokio, están esforzándose cada vez más por disfrutar de las ventajas de poder vivir en un medio ambiente agradable y nítido. Aunque con un cierto retraso, están también volviendo a descubrir de nuevo los méritos inherentes a las viejas tradiciones.

Los jóvenes arquitectos japoneses de hoy en día han aparcado el ego que sus antecesores trasladaban a sus diseños y se esfuerzan primordialmente en hacer realidad los sueños y deseos de su clientela.

La arquitectura japonesa tradicional había ya influenciado de forma notable a un buen número de grandes arquitectos como Le Corbusier o Frank Lloyd Wright. En la actualidad, los jóvenes arquitectos japoneses están buscando adaptar, bajo un diferente prisma y circunstancias, elementos de la arquitectura tradicional japonesa a su propio diseño y modo de vida.

Deseamos que la edición de este libro, cuyo objetivo es presentar el verdadero Tokio mediante casas y edificios ubicados en diferentes barrios de la metrópolis, pueda servir también de referencia para futuros proyectos de construcción en otras zonas urbanas del planeta.

In a quiet residential area located in Tokyo's Setagaya district, this house resembles nothing less than an exclusive members-only bar. The artist responsible for this setting is Yukio Hashimoto, an interior designer famous for his state-of-the-art restaurants and bars. The young bachelor who owns this house noticed the log counter of a fashionable bar in central Tokyo designed by Hashimoto and had the courage to commission him with the design of his residence. The whole place exudes an air of modernity combined with distinctively Japanese finishing touches. It is worth highlighting the "LEM" stool by the London-based Japanese designers Shin & Tomoko Azumi.

Die Fassade dieses Hauses in einer ruhigen Wohnlage im Viertel von Setagaya in Tokio erinnert an eine exklusive Bar mit Zutritt nur für Mitglieder. Der wegen seiner avantgardistischen Gestaltung von Restaurants und Bars berühmte und bekannte Innenarchitekt Yukio Hashimoto übernahm die Dekoration. Der junge Besitzer hatte sich entschieden, ihn aufgrund seiner Begeisterung für die von diesem entworfene Innengestaltung einer modernen Bar im Zentrum Tokios mit dem Design zu beauftragen. Das „Setagaya T-home" verbindet modernes Flair, das im Tresen, der ähnlich dem der Bar aus einem abgeästeten Baumstamm besteht, Trägern aus japanischer Pinie, Gittern aus Kastanie und einem Zen-inspirierten Innengarten zum Ausdruck kommt, mit dem Charme und der rustikalen Einfachheit der japanischer Ästhetik. Hervorzuheben wäre noch der Schemel „LEM", ein Werk der in London lebenden Designer Shin & Tomoko Azumi.

Quelque part, dans un quartier résidentiel tranquille de Setagaya, une circonscription de Tokyo, se trouve cette demeure aux allures de club privé. Yukio Hashimoto, un designer d'intérieur renommé pour ses bars et restaurants à la mode, est responsable de cette création. Le jeune célibataire propriétaire de cette maison, ayant remarqué le comptoir en bois d'un bar à la mode du centre de Tokyo conçu par Yukio, s'aventura à lui commander la conception de sa résidence. Tout le lieu dégage un air de modernité accompagné ça et là de touches japonaises. Il convient de mentionner le tabouret « LEM » des créateurs japonais, basés à Londres, Shin & Tomoko Azumi.

Esta casa, cuya fachada tiene la apariencia de un bar exclusivamente para socios, se encuentra en una tranquila zona residencial del barrio de Setagaya, en Tokio. La persona encargada de su realización ha sido Yukio Hashimoto, un conocido interiorista, famoso por el vanguardismo de los restaurantes y bares por él diseñados. Su joven propietario decidió aventurarse y encargar el diseño de su futura casa a Hashimoto después de haber podido apreciar el interiorismo de un moderno bar del centro de Tokio realizado por éste, en el que destacaba un particular mostrador en leño. El interiorismo de la Setagaya T-Home, aporta un aire de modernidad combinada con el encanto y sencillez rústica de la estética japonesa. Destaca también el taburete "LEM", obra de los diseñadores japoneses residentes en Londres Shin & Tomoko Azumi.

e-mail: hydesign@din.or.jp Photos: Hiroyuki Hirai Completion date: 2001

Hijiki, the name of the happy-looking cat in this house, is also the name of a type of seaweed often used in Japanese cooking. The house is located in Kunitachi, a famous university area, devoid of high-rise buildings and surrounded by a lot of greenery. The old and relaxed atmosphere of the past still endures in this Tokyo neighborhood. The married couple who rented the house are both architects and they have converted it into a space designed for living and working. Their lifestyle embodies the charm which is still so apparent in many of Tokyo's neighbourhoods and has survived the passing of time. It is a return to the life portrayed in Yasujiro Ozu's splendid films of the 1950s.

Hijiki, der Name der glücklichen Katze dieses Hauses, ist gleichzeitig der Name für eine in der japanischen Küche oft verwendeten Algenart. Das Haus liegt in Kunitachi, berühmt wegen seiner Universität. In dieser Gegend ohne hohe Gebäude, mit üppiger Vegetation und vielen Grünflächen empfindet man noch die entspannende, geruhsame und ruhige Atmosphäre des Tokio vergangener Zeiten. Die Bewohner, zwei Architekten, mieteten das Haus und renovierten es als Wohnung und Büro. Es verkörpert den noch spürbaren Charme vieler Viertel Tokios, denen die Zeit nichts anhaben konnte. Es ist wie eine Rückkehr zu dem Tokio der wunderbaren Filme von Yasujiro Ozu aus den fünfziger Jahren.

Hijiki, l'heureux chat de la maison, est aussi le nom d'une variété d'algue souvent utilisée en cuisine japonaise. La maison se trouve à Kunitachi, une zone universitaire connue, dépourvue de gratte-ciel et baignée de verdure. Ce quartier de Tokyo a su préserver l'atmosphère tranquille et surannée du passé. Ce couple marié d'architectes louait la demeure et l'a transformée en son lieu de vie et de travail. Le style de vie donne corps au charme encore visible de nombre de quartiers de Tokyo, immuables face au passage du temps. C'est un retour à la vie dépeinte dans les splendides films de Yasujiro Ozu, des années 50.

Hijiki, el nombre del feliz gato de esta casa, también es el nombre por el que se conoce a una de las variedades de algas tan usadas en la cocina japonesa. La casa se halla situada en el barrio de Kunitachi, famoso por su universidad. En esta zona, carente de edificios altos, de abundante vegetación y verde, perdura aún la atmósfera relajante, pausada y tranquila del Tokio de épocas pasadas. Esta pareja de arquitectos alquiló y reformó la casa con el fin de que pudiera ser utilizada como vivienda y oficina. Su modo de vida tipifica y encarna el encanto, tan visible aún, de muchos barrios de Tokio cuya fisonomía no ha cambiado con el paso del tiempo. Es como una vuelta a la vida del Tokio representado en las maravillosas películas de Yasujiro Ozu de los años cincuenta.

Hijiki House ● Shoji Terabayashi & Yoko Tanaka

e-mail: **terra@inv.co.jp** Photos: **Shoji Terabayashi** Completion date: **1950 (original construction)**

49

This is an example of the one-story public housing units built around 40 years ago; it is located near a magnificent park created at the time of Tokyo's 1964 Olympic Games. When Ms. Watanabe, who works as a food coordinator for specialist magazines, rented this old house all the interior was divided into various tatami-floored rooms, and she completely refurbished it by means of a simple and natural interior design. This space is also used by Watanabe as her private studio; here photographers take pictures that will be included in the cookery section of various magazines. This is the home of somebody who likes to live at her own pace and values small pleasures, like drinking tea with friends on her engawa (veranda).

Dies ist eines der einstöckigen, staatlich subventionierten Häuser, die während der sechziger Jahre gebaut wurden. Es steht in der Nähe eines anlässlich der Olympischen Spiele von 1964 in Tokio großzügig angelegten Parkes. Frau Watanabe, die als Ernährungskoordinatorin für Fachzeitschriften schreibt, mietete dieses alte Haus mit Tatami-Fußboden, um es später zu renovieren und neu zu dekorieren. Die Inneneinrichtung ist einfach und natürlich; Frau Watanabe benutzt diesen Raum auch als Arbeitsplatz zum Fotografieren ihrer Produkte für Veröffentlichungen im kulinarischen Teil verschiedener Fachzeitschriften. Diese Bewohnerin lebt ihr eigenes Leben und schätzt kleine Dinge wie z. B. auf der Engawa (Veranda) des Hauses mit ihren Freunden einen guten Tee zu trinken.

Voici l'une des auberges d'un étage, construite il y a près de 40 ans et située vers un magnifique parc, créé à l'occasion des Jeux Olympiques de Tokyo de 1964. Mme Watanabe, qui est coordinatrice culinaire pour des magazines de spécialités, a loué cette vielle maison, alors dotée d'un intérieur distribué en plusieurs salles de tatamis, et l'a complètement rénovée. Arborant un design intérieur simple et naturel, cet espace sert également à Mme Watanabe d'atelier privé, où les photographes prennent des clichés qui seront insérés dans les sections culinaires de diverses revues. L'occupante, qui apprécie son rythme de vie, accorde de la valeur à certains moments, comme boire le thé avec ses amis sur la véranda (engawa).

Esta es una de las casas de planta baja de protección oficial que se construyeron durante la década de los sesenta. Está ubicada cerca de un espléndido parque construido con motivo de la celebración de los Juegos Olímpicos de Tokio de 1964. La señora Watanabe, que coordina reportajes y escribe sobre temas culinarios para revistas del sector, alquiló esta vieja casa con suelo de tatami. Posteriormente llevó a cabo reformas y la redecoró. Con un interiorismo simple y natural, el espacio también es usado por Watanabe como lugar de trabajo en donde realiza fotografías de productos para la sección de gastronomía de varias revistas especializadas. Esta inquilina, a la que gusta vivir a su aire, valora pequeños placeres como el poder degustar un buen té en la galería o engawa de la casa junto a sus amigos.

e-mail: stand@d4.dion.ne.jp Photos: Naruyasu Nabeshima Completion date: 2001

In Japan's Edo period (1603-1868) Senju prospered as a staging post on the road to Nikko. The former warehouse which the architect and illustrator Eri Nakada uses as her studio is situated in this town, which still exudes some of the atmosphere of its past. Nowadays, as the number of places in the area with historical vestiges is fast decreasing, this remaining kura warehouse has come to be a precious asset. Originally built in 1810, the kura was converted into a house right after the Second World War; Nakada rented it three years ago and undertook extensive reforms, blending traditional and modern styles. Furniture by Eames set off this time-honored setting.

Während der Edo Epoche (1603-1868) florierte Senju als Poststadt auf dem Weg der Postkutschen nach Nikko. Das frühere Lager, das der Architektin und Illustratorin Eri Nakada als Werkstatt und Wohnung dient, steht in dieser Ortschaft, die noch an vergangene Zeiten erinnert. Da sich jedoch in der Gegenwart die Anzahl der geschichtsträchtigen Orte und Gebäude drastisch reduziert, ist das Lager „Kura" zu einem wertvollen Zeugnis vergangener Epochen geworden. Sein ursprünglicher Bau geht auf 1810 zurück und erst kurz nach dem Zweiten Weltkrieg wurde es zu einem traditionellen Wohnhaus. Nakada mietete es vor drei Jahren, renovierte es von Grund auf und kombiniert in seiner Inneneinrichtung eine Mischung aus Antikem und Modernem, wozu auch die Möbel von Eames gehören.

Au cours de l'ère Edo (1603-1868) au Japon, Senju prospéra comme relais de poste sur la route de Nikko. L'ancien entrepôt utilisé comme atelier par Eri Nakada, architecte et illustrateur, est situé dans cette ville, un cadre encore tout imprégné de l'atmosphère du passé. Aujourd'hui, les endroits aux reflets historiques se faisant plus rares, cet entrepôt « kura » est devenu un bien précieux. Sa construction originelle remontant à 1810, le « kura » a été converti en maison juste après la seconde guerre mondiale. Nakada le loua trois ans auparavant et le rénova de fond en comble, mariant tradition et modernisme. Des meubles Eames contrastent avec le lieu chargé d'histoire.

En el Japón de la época Edo (1603-1868), Senju prosperó como pueblo de postas para los correos que cubrían con toda diligencia su ruta en dirección a Nikko. Este antiguo almacén que Eri Nakada, arquitecta e ilustradora, utiliza como taller y vivienda, se halla en dicha población, lugar que aún permite evocar el ambiente del pasado. Sin embargo, en la actualidad, al haberse reducido drásticamente el número de lugares o edificios en donde poder apreciar los vestigios de la historia, este almacén kura se ha convertido con el tiempo en un valioso testimonio de épocas pasadas. Construido originalmente en 1810, el kura pasó a ser una vivienda tradicional apenas acabada la Segunda Guerra Mundial. Nakada lo alquiló hace tres años, reformándolo completamente e incorporando a su interiorismo una mezcla de lo antiguo con lo moderno. Los muebles de Eames pasan a formar parte de este hábitat.

e-mail: nakada1@bd5.so-net.ne.jp Photos: Yasuhiko Kawashima, HIII Completion date: 1810 (original construction)

This house, built according to the canons of traditional Japanese architecture, is suitable for holding formal tea ceremonies. Located in the city of Saitama, part of Greater Tokyo, it features a large entrance hall and a bench, which is indispensable for tea ceremonies, as it allows guests to remove their shoes and tidy themselves up before the ceremony begins. The designers from the Takatsuka Architects firm took their inspiration from the works of the famous novelist Junichiro Tanizaki (1886-1965) on Japanese culture, in particular his book "Inei Raisan" (The Eulogy of Shadows). The house creates an esthetic relationship between light, as provided by the shoji paper on windows and sliding doors, and shadow, as found in the "Tokonoma".

In diesem, nach den Regeln der traditionellen japanischen Architektur gebauten Haus, können Tee-Zeremonien zelebriert werden. Es liegt in Saitama, einem Außenbezirk von Tokio, und fällt durch seine weiträumige Eingangshalle und seine breite Bank auf, ein unentbehrliches Element für die ankommenden Gäste, um ihre Schuhe auszuziehen und sich für die Tee-Zeremonie vorzubereiten. Das Design der Architektenfirma Takatsuka hält sich an die Ausführungen des berühmten Novellisten Junichiro Tanizaki (1886-1965) über die japanische Kultur in seinem Buch „Inei Raisan" (Lob der Schatten). In diesem Haus spürt man die ästhetische Beziehung zwischen dem Licht, durch Shoji-Papier an Fenstern und Schiebetüren gemildert, und den Schatten aus der Vertiefung „Tokonoma".

La maison, respectant les canons de l'architecture japonaise traditionnelle, peut accueillir des réceptions formelles de cérémonie du thé. Située dans la cité de Saitama, proche du Grand Tokyo, cette maison arbore un grand hall d'entrée et un banc, éléments indispensables où les invités aux cérémonies du thé peuvent retirer leurs chaussures et se préparer avant le début de la cérémonie. La société Takatsuka Architects a conçu le lieu en respectant les écrits du célèbre auteur Junichiro Tanizaki (1886-1965) sur la culture japonaise, dans son livre « Inei Raisan » (Éloge l'ombre). La maison incorpore la relation esthétique entre la légèreté, offerte par le papier shoji sur les fenêtres et panneaux coulissants, et une ombre trouvée dans le « Tokonoma ».

Esta casa, construida siguiendo los cánones de la arquitectura tradicional japonesa, es apropiada para celebrar la ceremonia del té. Ubicada en la ciudad de Saitama, en las afueras de Tokio, destacan en ella su espacioso hall de entrada y su amplio banco, elementos indispensables para que los huéspedes que llegan puedan quitarse los zapatos y arreglarse antes de iniciar dar la ceremonia. La firma de arquitectos Takatsuka se inspiró en los escritos del famoso novelista japonés Junichiro Tanizaki (1886-1965) sobre cultura japonesa, especialmente su libro "Inei Raisan" (Elogio de las Sombras). En esta casa está presente también la relación estética entre las luces que propicia el papel shoji en ventanas y puertas correderas y las sombras que proporciona el hueco tokonoma.

e-mail: info@takasuka-architects.com Photos: Shogo Sato / Radius
Completion date: 1983

The architects extensively researched traditional Japanese architecture before designing this Western-style house, adapted to the special requirements of the Japanese lifestyle. In some respects, its interior is reminiscent of the work of Frank Lloyd Wright. Areas like Sanno and Magome in Tokyo's Ota district still contain houses similar to this one, built in the 1930s in an eclectic Japanese-Western mix. They were once homes to famous writers like Mishima and Tanizaki. In this particular house, it is worth mentioning the original and striking design of its tatami room.

Nach eingehendem Studium und sorgfältiger Untersuchung der traditionellen japanischen Architektur, haben die Architekten dieses Haus zwar im westlichen Stil, aber angepasst an die japanischen Besonderheiten geplant. In gewisser Weise erinnert das Innendesign an den architektonischen Stil von Frank Lloyd Wright. Viele ähnliche Häuser im Ota-Viertel in Tokio sind heute noch in der Umgebung von Sanno oder Magome zu finden. In den dreißiger Jahren erbaut, mit einer eklektischen Mischung aus japanischen und europäischen Stilen, zählten zu ihren Mietern berühmte Romanschreiber und Novellisten wie Mishima und Tanizaki. In diesem konkreten Haus muss das neuerungsfreudige und originelle Design des Tatami-Zimmers hervorgehoben werden.

Les architectes ayant étudié et recherché profondément l'architecture de style japonais traditionnelle, ils ont conçu une maison au style occidental adaptée aux particularités du Japon. Par certains aspects, son design intérieur nous rappelle le style architectural de Frank Lloyd Wright. Construites dans des zones comme Sanno et Magome dans les années 30, selon un style éclectique japonais et occidental et ayant accueillis de célèbres écrivains et romanciers comme Mishima et Tanizaki, nombre de maisons semblables à celle-ci demeurent encore de nos jours dans la circonscription tokyoïte de Ota. Pour cette maison particulière, il convient de mentionner le design novateur et original de la salle de tatami.

Los arquitectos, después de estudiar e investigar profundamente las características de la arquitectura tradicional japonesa, han diseñado esta casa de estilo occidental pero adaptada a las peculiaridades de Japón. En cierto modo su interiorismo nos recuerda vagamente al estilo arquitectónico preconizado por Frank Lloyd Wright. Muchas otras casas de características similares, también ubicadas en el barrio de Ota de Tokio, aún perduran hoy en día en zonas como Sanno o Magome. Construidas durante los años treinta e incorporando una ecléctica mezcla de estilo japonés y europeo, tuvieron como inquilinos a célebres escritores como Mishima o Tanizaki. De esta casa en concreto cabe destacar el diseño innovador y original de su habitación de tatami.

e-mail: **info@takasuka-architects.com**
Photos: **Shogo Sato / Radius** Completion date: **1992**

Jindaiji, a Buddhist temple built in 733 AD, is located in the city of Chofu, in the suburbs of Tokyo. The area now contains a sumptuous Sukiya-style house that holds a genuine tea-ceremony room and Japanese garden. Although these days most Japanese people consider this type of building unaffordable and therefore beyond their means, Takatsuka Architects are striving to broaden its appeal by refraining from using an excessive amount of costly materials, yet retaining as much as possible the elegant simplicity of the Sukiya style. After World War II, there has been a proliferation of convenient yet dull mass-produced housing in Japan. It is time to rediscover the new merits of traditional Japanese architecture.

Jindaiji, ein buddhistischer Tempel in Chofu an der Peripherie von Tokio, wurde im Jahr 733 erbaut. Heute fällt in dieser Umgebung eine luxuriöse Villa im Sukiya-Stil auf, die im Innenraum über ein unverfälschtes Zimmer für Tee-Zeremonien und über einen echten japanischen Garten verfügt. Obwohl die meisten Japaner heute der Meinung sind, dass dieser Stil zu aufwendig ist, will Takatsuka diese Vorstellung widerlegen und vermeidet nach Möglichkeit die Verwendung teurer Materialien, erhält aber zugleich die elegante Einfachheit dieses Sukiya-Stiles. Nach dem Zweiten Weltkrieg florierten in Japan bequeme Reihenhäuser ohne jeglichen Charme. Es ist an der Zeit, die unbestreitbaren Verdienste der traditionellen japanischen Architcktur wieder zu entdecken.

Jindaiji, un temple bouddhiste érigé en 733, est situé dans la ville de Chofu, dans la banlieue de Tokyo. Aujourd'hui, la zone accueille une somptueuse maison de style Sukiya abritant une véritable salle de cérémonie du thé et un jardin japonais. Bien que de nos jours la plupart des Japonais estiment de ce type de construction hors de prix et donc hors de leur portée, Takatsuka Architects luttent pour étendre leur intérêt en évitant de trop recourir à des matériaux coûteux, tout en préservant la simplicité élégante du style Sukiya, autant que possible. Après la deuxième guerre mondiale, le Japon a vu proliférer des logements de masse pratiques mais sans intérêt. Il est temps de redécouvrir les nouveaux mérites de l'ancienne architecture de style japonais.

Jindaiji, templo budista ubicado en la ciudad de Chofu, en la periferia del gran Tokio, fue construido en el año 733. En la actualidad destaca también de este vecindario una lujosa casa, de estilo sukiya, que posee en su interior una genuina habitación para la ceremonia del té así como un verdadero jardín japonés. Aunque hoy en día la creencia mayoritaria entre los japoneses es la de que este estilo de construcción resulta excesivamente caro, Takatsuka Architects trabaja para romper dicha imagen, evitando en lo posible el uso de materiales costosos, pero manteniendo los parámetros de elegante simplicidad de este estilo. Tras la Segunda Guerra Mundial proliferó en Japón la fabricación de casas en serie cómodas pero sin ningún atractivo. Sería hora ya de volver a descubrir los innegables méritos de la arquitectura tradicional japonesa.

e-mail: info@takasuka-architects.com Photos: Shogo Sato / Radius
Completion date: 1982

As the title of this flat suggests, its space can be changed, like a stage setting, by combining the adjustable black boxes that comprise the furniture in a
variety of ways, in order to make it adapt to the vision of a particular environment. This conceptual design allows the space to function like a spiritual retreat or a tea-ceremony room, enabling anyone living under the stress of city
life to regain his or her original self. The design of its interior has managed to
transform the vulgar exterior landscape into an elegant silhouette, thanks to
the combination of blinds and roller-screens. This space, blending spiritual
depth and simplicity, could well be a model for the houses of the twenty-first
century.

Wie der Name dieses Apartments vermuten lässt, gleichen seine wechselnden Räumlichkeiten einer Theaterbühne, die mit den schwarzkastigen läng-
lichen Möbeln zu jeder gewünschten Szene verändert werden kann. Das Konzept seines Designs lässt die Kreation eines Raumes für geistige Zuflucht
oder für die Zeremonie des Tee zu, der immer Entspannung und Erholung vom
Stress des Stadtlebens gewährt. Die gelungene Inneneinrichtung des "Scene", in der die vulgäre Landschaft von draußen zu einer eleganten Silhouette
wird, ist der intelligenten Kombination von Wandschirmen und aufrollbaren
Stores zu verdanken. Dieser Raum, der Geistigkeit und Einfachheit vereint, wäre gut als das Modellhaus des 21. Jahrhunderts denkbar.

Comme le suggère le titre de l'appartement, son espace est évolutif tel un décor de théâtre, en combinant de diverses façons les meubles modulables en
forme de boîte noire, afin de l'adapter aux scènes de la vie particulière. Ce design conceptuel permet à l'espace de fonctionner en refuge spirituel, voire en
salle pour la cérémonie du thé permettant aux victimes du stress de la vie ur-
baine de retrouver un moi originel. Le design des intérieurs est une réussite,
conférant au simple paysage extérieur une silhouette élégante, en mariant stores et persiennes. Cet espace, mêlant heureusement profondeur et simplicité, pourrait se révéler une maison modèle du XXIème siècle.

Tal como el nombre de este apartamento sugiere, su espacio cambiante, como si de un escenario teatral se tratara, permite realizar diferentes combina-
ciones mediante el mobiliario ajustable en forma de caja negra alargada, para crear un espacio vital o escena deseados. Su diseño conceptual contribuye
a que se pueda dar el ambiente adecuado para realizar las funciones de refugio espiritual o servir como habitación para la ceremonia del té en donde
uno se recoge y recupera del estrés de la vida urbana. El logrado interiorismo
de Scene, en donde el paisaje vulgar del exterior se transforma en una elegante silueta, se consigue gracias a la combinación inteligente de persianas
con estores. Este espacio, que integra espiritualidad y simplicidad, podría bien
ser la casa modelo del siglo XXI.

e-mail: t-takuma@gray.plala.or.jp Photos: Nacása & Partners Completion date: 2000

SCENE 1 - Table and bench

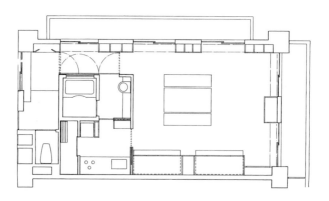

SCENE 3 - Bedroom

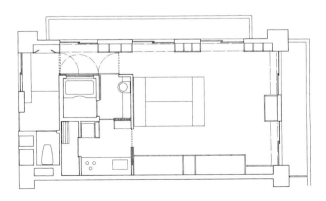

SCENE 4 - Party

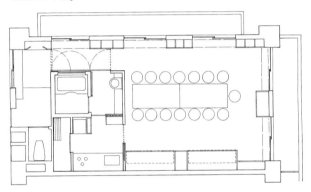

SCENE 5 - Gallery

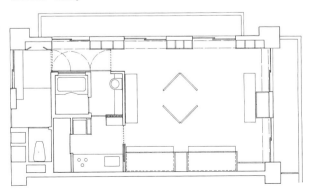

SCENE 2 - Tea Ceremony

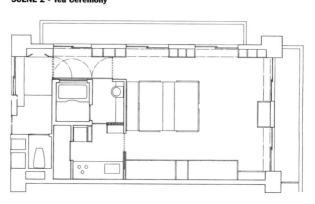

The interior designer Hiroshi Seki always seems to manage to find the right materials for a particular setting, in keeping with their function and importance. Mainly active in the field of shop design, with brand names like Jigsaw or Jürgen Lehl among his customers, Seki is also known for his collaboration with the distinguished British architect John Pawson. This is Seki's own home, located in the Nakano district, an area in central Tokyo to the west of Shinjuku. After closely examining the space available, Seki concerned himself with even the tiniest details, and his pursuit of beauty in the most commonplace item resulted in a house full of simplicity, functionality and charm.

In Harmonie mit Bedeutung und Funktion eines konkreten Raumes gelingt es dem Innenarchitekten Hiroshi Seki immer wieder, das passende Material für einen spezifische Raum zu finden. Obwohl sich Seki hauptsächlich mit dem Design von Läden beschäftigt und zu seinen Kunden geschätzte Marken wie Jigsaw oder Jürgen Lehl und andere gehören, kennt man ihn auch durch seine aktive Zusammenarbeit mit dem berühmten englischen Architekten John Pawson. Dies ist sein Haus in Nakano im Westen von Shinjuku im Zentrum Tokios. Nach eingehender Untersuchung des Raumes für seine zukünftige Wohnung verwandte er große Sorgfalt auf die kleinsten Details und schuf so ein Haus, dessen größte Attraktion Einfachheit und Funktionalität sind.

En harmonie avec les sens et fonctions des divers espaces, le créateur d'intérieur Hiroshi Seki sait trouver les matériaux s'adaptant exactement à une réalité précise. Actif surtout dans la création de boutiques, pour des noms comme Jigsaw ou Jürgen Lehl, Seki est aussi connu pour son travail avec le célèbre architecte britannique John Pawson. Il s'agit de sa demeure, située dans la circonscription de Nakano, une zone à l'ouest de Shinjuku, au centre de Tokyo. Le designer, après un examen minutieux de l'espace de cet appartement résidentiel, a traité particulièrement attentivement chaque détail, créant dans sa quête de la beauté ordinaire une maison pleine de simplicité, de fonctionnalité et de charme.

De acuerdo con el significado y función de un espacio concreto, Hiroshi Seki, interiorista, consigue siempre encontrar el material adecuado a una realidad específica. Básicamente dedicado al diseño de interiores de tiendas, y teniendo como clientes a marcas tan reputadas como Jigsaw o Jürgen Lehl entre otras, Seki es también conocido por haber colaborado activamente con el célebre arquitecto británico John Pawson. Ésta, su casa, se halla ubicada en el barrio de Nakano, al oeste de Shinjuku, en el centro de Tokio. El diseñador, una vez examinado detenidamente el espacio destinado a ser su futura residencia, prestó una exhaustiva atención al más mínimo detalle, logrando de este modo sintetizar un estilo de casa cuyo mayor atractivo reside en la simplicidad y funcionalidad.

e-mail: s.e.k.l@siren.ocn.ne.jp   Photos: Satoshi Asakawa   Completion date: 2001

The house of Katushi Nagumo, a designer whose work ranges from furniture and objects to landscapes, is situated in Hino city, on the outskirts of Greater Tokyo. Despite the ugliness of Tokyo's periphery, with its densely built-up areas, Nagumo has said that he chose these surroundings because, as a native of the mountainous Niigata region, they provide him with a nostalgic view of Mount Fuji and the peaks of the Hakone mountains. Even though this is a small 2-story house, with a floor space of only 750 square feet, Nagumo decided to give over a generous proportion – 430 square feet – to the spacious living room. The furniture, made up of attractive, mobile pieces designed by Nagumo himself, was inspired by ancient Japanese tales.

Das Haus von Katushi Nagumo, eines Designers für Möbel und Produkte sowie Landschaftsarchitekten, befindet sich in Hino, in den Außenbezirken von Tokio. Trotz des wenig attraktiven Stadtbildes an der Peripherie dieser Stadt wählte Nagumo diese Gegend für den Bau seines Hauses, um von hier aus den Fuji und die Gipfel der Hakone-Kette zu bewundern, die ihn an seine heimatliche Provinz Niigata erinnern. Dieser originelle und großzügige Designer richtete sich in diesem 70 m^2 großen Haus ein weiträumiges Wohnzimmer von 40m^2 ein. Inspiriert durch alte japanische Erzählungen entwirft Nagumo sein eigenes Mobiliar aus interessanten beweglichen Teilen.

La maison de Katushi Nagumo, créateur de mobilier et de produits jusqu'au paysagisme, se trouve à Hino city, à la lisière de la grande Tokyo. En dépit d'un paysage urbain périphérique sans grâce, avec ses zones de construction denses, le créateur est réputé avoir choisi ce cadre parce que, natif de la région montagneuse de Niigata, il peut se laisser aller à la contemplation de la ligne de crête des monts Fuji et Hakone. Même si la petite maison compte seulement deux étages et 70 mètres carrés, le designer a décidé, en toute magnanimité, de consacrer 40 mètres carrés à son spacieux séjour. Le mobilier de la demeure, composé de pièces similaires et mobiles, est l'œuvre de Nagumo lui-même, qui a puisé son inspiration dans les anciens contes japonais.

La casa de Katushi Nagumo, diseñador de muebles, productos y paisajes, se halla en la ciudad de Hino, en las afueras del gran Tokio. A pesar del terrible paisajismo urbano de la periferia de esta ciudad con su alta densidad de zonas urbanizadas, Nagumo escogió este área para construir su casa por el hecho de que desde la misma se puede aún contemplar con facilidad el monte Fuji y las crestas de las montañas de Hakone, paisaje que, a su vez, le recuerda vagamente al de su provincia natal de Niigata. Este diseñador, con actitud desprendida y magnánima, optó por invertir 40 de los 70 m^2 de que consta esta pequeña casa en crear una espaciosa sala de estar. Asimismo, inspirándose en cuentos del Japón de la antigüedad, Nagumo diseñó también su propio mobiliario, compuesto de interesantes piezas móviles.

e-mail: nagumo@nagumo-design.com Photos: Nagumo Design Completion date: 1992

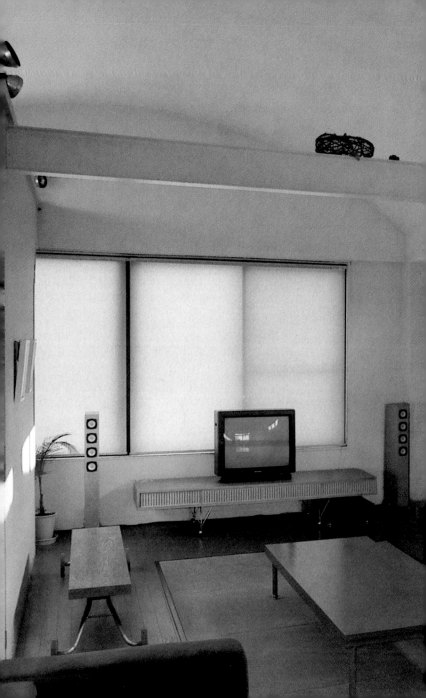

Following the wishes of the owner of this house, who wanted to live surrounded by his favourite things, the architect built this four-level building in the Meguro district of central Tokyo. The house is occupied by five people, who make up two separate households: a married working couple in their 40s with a child on the one hand, and the husband's parents, in their 60s, who still run a motorbike shop, on the other. The young husband, a men's fashion designer, also has his own workshop on the top floor of this building. The house, intended as both a work space and a residence, boasts an unusual selection of electrical sockets, doorknobs and other objects, all carefully chosen by the owner himself.

Den Wünschen des Eigentümers dieses Hauses entsprechend, erbaute der Architekt in Meguro, im Zentrum von Tokio, dieses Gebäude auf vier Ebenen, damit der Besitzer sich hier mit seinen Lieblingsobjekten umgeben konnte. In dem Gebäude leben fünf Personen in zwei Haushalten. Der eine besteht aus einem berufstätigen, etwa vierzigjährigen Ehepaar mit einem Sohn, und der andere aus den sechzigjährigen Eltern des Ehemannes, den Besitzern eines Motorradladens. Der Ehemann ist Designer für Herrenmode und arbeitet in seiner eigenen Werkstatt im obersten Stockwerk des Gebäudes. Das Haus, das als Privatwohnung und Arbeitsplatz konzipiert wurde, überrascht durch eine Reihe sehenswerter Schalterplatten, Türgriffe und anderer, von seinem Besitzer sorgfältig ausgewählter, Gegenstände.

Respectant les vœux du propriétaire, vivre au milieu de ses objets favoris, l'architecte a construit cet édifice de quatre niveaux dans le quartier de Meguro, au centre de Tokyo. La maison accueille cinq personnes, formant deux foyers séparés. Un couple marié dans leur quarantaine avec un enfant et les parents du mari, ayant passé soixante ans, qui tiennent toujours un magasin de motos. Le jeune mari, un créateur de mode masculine, dispose également de son propre atelier au dernier étage de la maison. Celle-ci, conçue comme un lieu de travail et de vie abrite tout un éventail d'interrupteurs, de boutons de porte et d'objets choisis avec soin par le propriétaire lui-même.

Dando cumplimiento a los deseos del propietario de esta casa, el arquitecto construyó este edificio de cuatro niveles en el barrio de Meguro, en el centro de Tokio, para que éste pudiera vivir rodeado de sus objetos más preciados. El edificio está habitado por cinco personas distribuidas en dos unidades familiares. Una compuesta por un matrimonio de profesionales, de unos cuarenta años, con un hijo, y otra compuesta por los padres del marido, de unos 60 años, propietarios de una tienda de motocicletas. El marido, diseñador de moda masculina, tiene el taller en la parte superior del mismo inmueble. La casa ideada como residencia particular y lugar de trabajo alberga también toda una particular y curiosa serie de placas de interruptores, tiradores de puertas y demás objetos cuidadosamente seleccionados y escogidos por su propietario.

e-mail: taller@ci.mbn.or.jp Photos: Nacása & Partners Completion date: 1993

This house lies in a densely populated area near Shimokitazawa, crammed with narrow houses lining both sides of the street; it is home to the architect Matsunaga. When designing his house, Matsunaga deliberately rejected blending the idiosyncrasies of the surroundings with the interior design. Instead, he created a space in the heart of the building, like an inner courtyard, with a transparent roof to give an open-air effect. As a result, each room of the house serves the additional function of being a kind of balcony overlooking the inner patio, giving rise to an open and cheerful atmosphere for the inhabitants.

In dieser dichtbevölkerten Gegend in der Nähe von Shimokitazawa, eines zentralen Viertels von Tokio, mit seinen kleinen und engen Häusern, lebt der Architekt Matsunaga. Beim Entwurf dieses Projektes hat der Architekt bewusst auf die Möglichkeit verzichtet, den Eigencharakter des umgebenden Stadtbildes in die Inneneinrichtung des Hauses zu integrieren. Matsunaga entschied sich für einen Innenhof im Zentrum des Gebäudes, mit einer hohen, durchscheinenden Decke, die das Gefühl vermittelt, im Freien zu sein. Durch die rundherum angeordneten Zimmer können sich die Bewohner einer allgemein frischen und freundlichen Atmosphäre erfreuen.

Dans la zone densément peuplée de Shimokitazawa, le quartier de M. Matsunaga, un architecte, est rempli à l'envi de maisons étroites bordant chaque côté de la rue. En concevant cette demeure, Matsunaga a voulu marquer une rupture avec les particularismes environnants par le design intérieur de la maison. Il a plutôt préféré disposer un faux espace ouvert ressemblant à un patio intérieur avec un toit transparent, au centre même de la construction. Ainsi, chaque pièce peut se transformer en un balcon supplémentaire surplombant le patio intérieur, générant une atmosphère vive et joyeuse dans la vie quotidienne des habitants.

Esta casa, donde reside el arquitecto Matsunaga, está en una parte bastante central de Tokio, en un barrio atestado de casas pequeñas y estrechas, con una altísima densidad de población, cerca de Shimokitazawa. Al diseñar este proyecto, el arquitecto prescindió de forma voluntaria de la posibilidad de incorporar la idisiosincracia del paisaje de este vecindario al interiorismo de la casa. Matsunaga optó más bien por emplazar en el centro del edificio un patio interior cubierto por un tejado alto y transparente que transmite una sensación de espacio al aire libre. Con las habitaciones ubicadas alrededor del mismo, los habitantes de esta casa pueden gozar de un ambiente general fresco y alegre.

e-mail: clip@mp.0038.net Photos: Clip Completion date: 2001

This house designed by Takashi Iwama is situated near Haneda airport, by the river Tamagawa that divides the cities of Tokyo and Kawasaki. The soft soil and the resulting difficulties in putting up a large building on it were the factors that determined the light steel frame structure chosen by the architect. The fourth floor, on the top, with its spacious bathroom and terrace, is a response to the owner's desire to take advantage of the view and the cool breezes coming from the Tamagawa river. In the well-tended gardens on both sides of the Tamagawa, the locals revel in the surroundings by playing soccer, baseball, golf, going jogging, etc.

In der Nähe des Flughafens von Haneda, mit Blick auf den Fluss Tamagawa, der die Städte Tokio und Kawasaki voneinander trennt, liegt dieses von Takashi Iwama entworfene Haus. Infolge des weichen Bodens entschied sich der Architekt bei der Konstruktion für eine leichte Stahlstruktur. In der vierten und letzten Etage befindet sich das Bad und eine Terrasse, von der aus der Besitzer die angenehme Brise vom Fluss her genießen kann. Am Fuße des Flusses Tamagawa können die Bewohner von Tokio und Kawasaki an den gepflegten und bepflanzten Ufern die herrliche Landschaft genießen, Fußball, Baseball oder Golf spielen, joggen, etc.

Conçue par Takashi Iwama, cette maison est proche de l'aéroport de Haneda, près de la rivière Tamagawa séparant les cités de Tokyo et de Kawasaki. Le sol meuble des fondations de la parcelle et les difficultés d'y ériger une construction lourde et massive sont à l'origine de la structure légère en acier de la construction choisie par l'architecte. Le quatrième, une demande spéciale du propriétaire souhaitant profiter de la vue et de la brise venant de la rivière Tamagawa, abrite un bain spacieux et une terrasse. À la lisière de la rivière, le long des jardins soignés de ses deux rives, chacun peut profiter du cadre pour jouer au football, au baseball, au golf ou simplement courir.

Esta casa diseñada por Takashi Iwama está cerca del aeropuerto de Haneda y tiene vistas sobre el río Tamagawa, el cual delimita las ciudades de Tokio y Kawasaki. Debido a las características del terreno, de suelo blando, el arquitecto optó por utilizar una estructura ligera de acero en su construcción. El último y cuarto piso continene un baño y una terraza desde donde se disfruta de la agradable brisa procedente del río. Al pie del río Tamagawa, y a lo largo de sus bien cuidadas y ajardinadas orillas, los habitantes de Tokio y Kawasaki pueden gozar de este bello paraje practicando fútbol, baseball, golf, jogging, etcétera.

e-mail: iwama@socius.co.jp Photos: Takashi Iwama Completion date: 1998

Mikan, an exciting architectural studio formed by Kiwako Kamo, Masashi Sogabe, Masayuki Takeuchi and Manuel Tardits, has captured the attention on many young Japanese architects, with renowned projects such as the NHK Nagano Broadcasting Station, and the Issey Miyake shop in Daikanyama. This particular house was built in a residential area in Tokyo's Meguro district for a couple and their two young children. The project is a fluid composition of juxtaposed spaces, separated by sliding doors and closed off by a set of enormous sliding wood panels. These panels satisfy the demands of privacy and the control of light, as well as providing an ever-changing facade, in contrast to the rigid box-like form.

Mikan, ein charismatisches Architektenstudio, zu dem Kiwako Kamo, Masashi Sogabe, Masayuki Takeuchi und Manuel Tradits gehören, ist mit seinen bekannten Projekten wie NHK Broadcasting Station oder dem Laden von Issey Miyake in Daikanyama, eine Quelle der Inspiration und Anregung für die neue Generation der japanischen Architekten. Dieses besondere Haus wurde für ein Ehepaar mit zwei Kindern in der Wohngegend des Viertels Meguro in Tokio gebaut. Das Projekt ist eine ineinanderübergehende Komposition nebeneinandergestellter Räume, getrennt durch Schiebetüren und abgeschlossen durch große Holzpaneele, die gleichzeitig Intimität schaffen, das Licht kontrollieren und Ausdruck einer ewig wechselnden Fassade im Gegensatz zur Steifheit des kastenförmigen Hauses sind.

Mikan, une étude d'architecte inspirée formée par Kiwako Kamo, Masashi Sogabe, Masayuki Takeuchi et Manuel Tardits, captive l'attention des jeunes architectes japonais par des projets de renom comme la Station d'émission de Nagano de la NHK, et la boutique Issey Miyake de Daikanyama. Cette demeure particulière a été construite dans une zone résidentielle de Meguro, une circonscription de Tokyo, pour un couple et ses deux jeunes enfants. Le projet est une composition fluide d'espaces juxtaposés, séparés par des portes coulissantes et fermés par un ensemble de cloisons de bois géantes et coulissantes. Ces panneaux satisfont tant la vie privée, que le contrôle de la lumière et l'expression d'une façade évoluant sans cesse en contraste avec la forme rigide du cadre.

Mikan es un carismático estudio de arquitectura formado por Kiwako Kamo, Masashi Sogabe, Masayuki Takeuchi y Manuel Tardits. Proyectos de renombre como la NHK de Nagano Broadcasting Station, o la tienda Issey Miyake en Daikanyama son también un foco de inspiración y éstimulo para nuevas generaciones de arquitectos japoneses. Esta casa en cuestión se construyó para un matrimonio y sus dos hijos en una zona residencial del barrio de Meguro en Tokio. El proyecto es una composición fluida de espacios yuxtapuestos, separados por puertas correderas y cerrados a través de grandes paneles de madera. Éstos sirven también para dar intimidad, para controlar el nivel de luz y como expresión de una fachada cambiante en contraposición a la rigidez de la casa en forma de caja.

e-mail: info@mikan.co.jp Photos: Covi Completion date: 2002

This house, conceived as an addition to a previously existing one, was built for a married couple and their children in a popular Tokyo neighborhood. The square-shape plot, the need to maintain a relationship with the older building while benefiting from its own entrance and finally, the client's very specific functional requirements all led Mikan to devise this bare concrete and simple form. The house is vertically organized, with each floor envisaged as an almost independent unit. All the space containing the fluidly connected kitchen, lounge and dining room has been placed in the cantilevered structure to compensate for the lack of natural light on this confined piece of land. This floor is also connected to the old house by means of an overpass.

Das Haus, konzipiert als Anbau eines bereits bestehenden Gebäudes, wurde für eine Familie mit Kindern in einem populären Viertel von Tokio gebaut. Mikan entwarf diese einfach strukturierte Betonkonstruktion und entsprach damit dem Wunsch des Kunden nach einer asketischen und funktionellen Gestaltung mit direktem Zugang. Die Struktur des Hauses ist vertikal ausgerichtet, so dass jedes Stockwerk eine unabhängige Einheit bildet. Der Raum mit durchgehender Verbindung zwischen Küche, Esszimmer und Wohnzimmer befindet sich auf dem überkragenden Teil der Struktur auf einem freitragenden Träger, um das auf diesem engen Grund so nötige Tageslicht hereinzulassen. Das Obergeschoss ist ebenfalls mit dem alten Gebäude über eine Überführung verbunden.

La maison, une extension de la demeure existante, a été construite pour un couple marié et ses enfants, dans une partie du Tokyo populaire. La parcelle carrée de terrain, le besoin de préserver la relation avec l'ancienne maison tout en créant un accès indépendant et, enfin, les exigences fonctionnelles et esthétiques très spécifiques du client, ont conduit Mikan à concevoir ce volume simple de béton nu. La maison est ordonnée verticalement, chaque niveau envisagé pratiquement comme une unité superposée indépendante. L'ensemble de l'espace, une connexion fluide entre cuisine, séjour et salle à manger, est situé dans le volume en porte-à-faux, en raison de la soif de lumière de ce terrain étroit. Le sol est aussi relié à l'ancienne demeure par une passerelle.

Esta casa, concebida como una parte adicional a la ya existente previamente, se construyó en un barrio popular de Tokio para una familia con hijos. Mikan diseñó una construcción de hormigón de estructura simple, unida a la antigua, pero dando respuesta al deseo del cliente de obtener un espacio ascético, funcional y al cual se pudiera acceder de forma directa. La casa está estructurada verticalmente de forma que casa piso funciona como una unidad independiente. Todo el espacio que alberga la fluida conexión entre cocina, comedor y salón se halla ubicado en la parte de la estructura voladiza, con el fin de poder captar la luz natural de la que está necesitado este apretado solar. El piso superior está también conectado con el edificio antiguo mediante te un paso elevado.

e-mail: info@mikan.co.jp Photos: Covi Completion date: 2001

Cesar Pelli, a world-famous architect, renowned for having designed the TWA terminal at the JFK international airport in New York, supervised of the interior design of the Forest Tower complex. In this 42-story tower, a "natural" concept has been applied to interiors. Natural spaces exude warmth, with contrasting wooden walls, carefully selected stone materials and man-made fabrics creating a beautiful finish. The wooded area dotted with temples and shrines for centuries in which the tower stands provides residents with stunning views of the city at its highest point, the Green Hills spa, at an altitude of 460 feet.

Der weltberühmte Architekt Cesar Pelli, ganz besonders bekannt durch sein Projekt für das Terminal der TWA im JFK Flughafen von New York, überwachte persönlich die Inneneinrichtung des Forest Tower Komplexes. In diesem Hochhaus mit 42 Stockwerken führte Pelli für die Innendekoration ein Konzept der „Natürlichkeit" ein. Schlichte Räume die Wärme ausstrahlen, Wände aus Holz, sorgfältig ausgewählte Steine und Marmor sowie Naturstoffe heben die harmonische Ausstattung hervor. Der Forest Tower steht inmitten eines Waldes mit jahrhundertealten Tempeln und Heiligtümern. Von oben können die Bewohner in 140 Meter Höhe vom Green Hills Spa aus spektakuläre Ausblicke über die Stadt genießen.

Cesar Pelli, architecte de renommée mondiale, célèbre pour la conception du terminal TWA de l'aéroport international JFK de New York, a supervisé la conception intérieure du complexe de la Tour Forest. Un concept « naturel » a été appliqué aux intérieurs de cette tour de 42 étages. Les espaces naturels dégagent une chaleur contrastant avec les murs boisés, les pierres choisies avec soin et des surfaces en tissu, soulignant une superbe finition. De la zone boisée, étudiée depuis des siècles par des temples et des chapelles, où se dresse la tour, les résidents peuvent jouir de vues saisissantes de la ville à la source de Green Hills, à 140 mètres au-dessus du sol.

Cesar Pelli, arquitecto conocido en todo el mundo por, entre otros proytectos, su diseño de la terminal TWA en el aeropuerto JFK de Nueva York, dirigió y supervisó personalmente el interiorismo del complejo Forest Tower. En el diseño de los interiores de esta torre de 42 plantas, Pelli introduce el elemento de "lo natural" de forma generalizada. Espacios naturales que rezuman ambientes cálidos, paredes de madera, materiales en piedra y mármol cuidadosamente seleccionados, y auténticas telas y tejidos naturales contribuyen a realzar su hermoso acabado. La Forest Tower está en medio de un área boscosa en la que destacan los templos y santuarios desde tiempos inmemoriales. En su parte más elevada, a 140 metros de altura, se halla el balneario Green Hills, desde donde sus inquilinos pueden disfrutar de espectaculares vistas sobre la ciudad.

http://rvww.mori.co.jp/residence Completion date: 2001

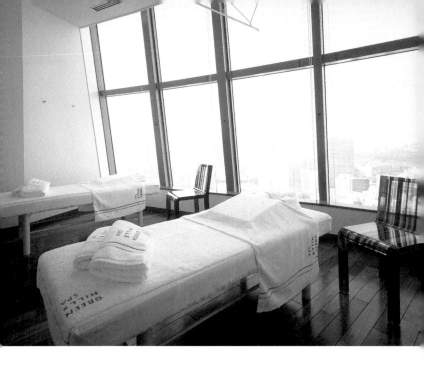

A bird´s eye view

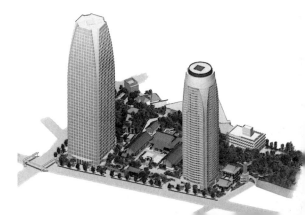

Living comfortably right in the heart of Tokyo, relishing the prospect of gaining full access to an extensive range of services, from concierge facilities to round-the-clock security on the premises: this is the concept behind Moto Azabu Hills. Surrounded by greenery, this project was designed by Shozo Uchii. Conran & Partners, designed three types of apartments. The main style, known as "Hidden Beauty", conceals 4 types of secret mechanisms: Color Appearance, Surprise Function, Lightning Effect, and Change of View. As doors open onto spaces partitioned with walnut and glass screens, the residents enter into a startling new dimension, abounding in color and sensations.

Komfortables Leben mitten in Tokio, mit Anspruch auf eine große Auswahl von Dienstleistungen, vom Pförtner bis zum Sicherheitsdienst rund um die Uhr, das ist das Konzept von Moto Azabu Hills. Das Design des Projektes inmitten einer großflächigen Grünzone stammt von Shozo Uchii. Conran & Partners, entwarf drei Apartment-Prototypen. Unter den verschiedenen Varianten der angewandten Innendekorationen ist die sogenannte „Hidden Beauty" hervorzuheben, die folgende geheime Facetten verbirgt: Farbe, Überraschungseffekt, Beleuchtungseffekt und Blickfeldwechsel. Die Innendekoration von „Hidden Beauty" öffnet dem Bewohner Zugang zu neuen und besonderen Dimensionen, reichhaltig an Farben und Eindrücken.

Vivre confortablement au cœur de Tokyo, jouir d'un accès complet à toute une gamme de services, d'une conciergerie à une sécurité H24 dans les installations, tel est le concept derrière Moto Azabu Hills. Baignée de verdure, cette tour est la création de Shozo Uchii. Conran & Partners, a conçu trois types d'appartements. Le style principal d'intérieur, connu comme « Hidden Beauty » , abrite 4 types de mécanismes secrets : Couleur apparente, Fonction surprise, Jeu de lumière et Changement de vue. Les portes s'ouvrent sur des espaces aux partitions de noyer et de verre et les habitants pénètrent une autre dimension, riche en couleurs et sensations.

Moto Azabu Hills proporciona a sus residentes la posibilidad de acceder a una amplia gama de servicios integrados, desde conserjería a un servicio de seguridad operativo las 24 horas del día, así como el placer de poder disfrutar de un estilo de vida comfortable en pleno centro de Tokio. Shozo Uchii diseñó éste proyecto, ubicado en medio de una gran zona verde. Conran & Partners planificó tres tipos de apartamentos. De entre las diferentes variantes de interiorismo aplicadas, destaca la denominada "Hidden Beauty", que esconde las siguientes facetas: Apariencia de Colores, Función Sorprendente, Efecto Luminoso, y Cambio de Vista. El interiorismo de "Hidden Beauty" permite al residente entrar en una nueva y particular dimensión, rica en colores y sensaciones.

http://www.mori.co.jp/residence Completion date: 2002

Floor Plan "Hidden Beauty"

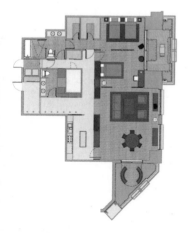

The private home of the architect Makoto Tanaka is distinctive for the three cylinders inside the building. The house is located in a quiet residential area in Tokyo's Setagaya district. The designer seems to have been attracted by these circular columns because they remind him of a tree, stripped down to its basic form, as well as evoking symbols and defining a vertical thrust. The cylinders serve as a kitchen, a bathroom, a toilet and even a stairway. They have the capacity of being both an open and a closed space at the same time, in the manner of the Ying and Yang. They encourage activity on the part of the people living in the house.

Die Hauptattraktion im Privathaus des Architekten Makoto Tanaka sind die drei Zylinder in seinem Inneren. Das Gebäude liegt in einer ruhigen Wohnlage im Viertel von Setagaya in Tokio. Der Designer fühlte sich von den runden Säulen angezogen, die ihn an die ursprüngliche Form des Baumes erinnern und ihm Symbolik und Vertikalität übermitteln. Die Zylinder übernehmen im Haus vielfältige Funktionen, so dient ihr Raum zur Unterbringung von Küche, Bad, Waschbecken und sogar der Treppe nach oben. Die Zylinder sind gleichzeitig offener und geschlossener Raum und beschwören die Beziehung zwischen dem Ying und dem Yang herauf. Ein Raum der Bewegung und der Aktivität für die darin lebenden Personen.

La résidence privée de l'architecte Makoto Tanaka a pour originalité distinctive d'abriter trois cylindres en son sein. Cette maison se niche dans la zone résidentielle tranquille de Setagaya, un district de Tokyo. Le créateur semble avoir été attiré par ces colonnes qui lui rappellent la forme originelle d'un arbre, tout en suggérant un certain symbolisme, et la verticalité. Dans la maison, les cylindres abritent une cuisine, une salle de bain, des toilettes et même un escalier. Ils offrent la capacité d'être à la fois des espaces fermés et ouverts, comme dans une relation Ying/Yang. Ils deviennent un espace induisant une action, une activité de ses habitants.

Los tres cilindros colocados en el interior de la casa particular del arquitecto Makoto Tanaka conforman su principal característica. El edificio se halla en una tranquila zona residencial situada en el barrio Setagaya de Tokio. El diseñador parece sentirse atraído por las columnas circulares, ya que le recuerdan al árbol en su forma original. Estas le sugieren también conceptos de simbolismo y verticalidad. La función asignada a los cilindros dentro de la casa es variada, siendo utilizados como espacio para albergar la cocina, el baño, el lavabo o incluso la escalera que conduce al piso superior. Los cilindros actúan como un espacio abierto y cerrado a la vez, evocando la relación entre el yin y el yan. Un espacio que provoca la acción y la actividad de las personas que en él habitan.

Photos: **Makoto Tanaka** Completion date: **2001**

Section

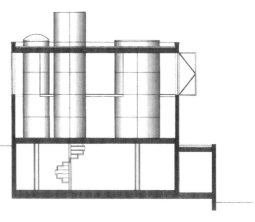

165

The architect Tatsuo Iwaoka spent a full 6 months studying possible sites for his house in the Ginza area of Tokyo's central district. He finally discovered a long, narrow plot in between a Chinese noodle shop and a sushi restaurant. This small piece of land seemed to be overshadowed by its surrounding high-rise buildings. However, Iwaoka sensed the infinite possibilities of this narrow strip of land and therefore decided to purchase it. He achieved a sensation of openness by creating an inner courtyard on the second story of the three-leveled structure. In stark contrast to the colossal building projects underway in central Tokyo, Iwaoka has succeeded in creating a very inviting home on a human scale.

Der Architekt Tatsuo Iwaoka suchte volle 6 Monate in der Umgebung von Ginza in Tokios zentralem Vorort „Chuo" nach einem geeigneten Platz für sein zukünftiges Haus. Endlich fand er ein schmales langes Grundstück neben einem Laden für chinesische Nudeln und einem „Sushi"-Restaurant. Diese kleine Parzelle inmitten der hohen Gebäude schien der Vergessenheit anzugehören, doch er spürte seine unermesslichen Möglichkeiten und erwarb das Grundstück. Auf der zweiten Ebene des auf drei Ebenen verteilten Innenraums schuf er einen offenen Hof, der Weite und Geräumigkeit vermittelt. In eindeutigem Kontrast zu den heute im Zentrum von Tokio üblichen monumentalen Konstruktionen schafft Iwaoka ein zurückhaltendes Werk mit menschlichen Proportionen.

L'architecte Tatsuo Iwaoka a passé 6 mois entiers à étudier et rechercher des sites possibles autour de la zone de Ginza dans Chuo, la circonscription centrale de Tokyo. Il a finalement découvert un espace étroit et long, entre une boutique de nouilles chinoises et un restaurant de sushi. Ce recoin semblait condamné à l'oubli au cœur d'une zone toute de grands édifices. Il perçut les potentialités infinies de cette langue de terrain et décida de se porter acquéreur de la parcelle. Il généra une sensation d'ouverture en créant une cour intérieure au deuxième étage de structure qui en comptait trois. En contraste saisissant au caractère colossal et gigantesque des projets du centre de Tokyo, Iwaoka réussit à créer une œuvre superbe, décente et à échelle humaine.

El arquitecto Tatsuo Iwaoka invirtió seis meses completos en la búsqueda de un emplazamiento para su futura casa en la zona de Ginza del distrito central de Tokio, Chuo. Finalmente descubrió un largo y estrecho solar entre un local que sirve fideos chinos y un restaurante de sushi. Esta pequeña parcela rodeada de edificios altos parecía predestinada al olvido. Intuyendo sus infinitas posibilidades, la adquirió. En el segundo nivel de una estructura de interiores a tres niveles, creó un patio abierto que proporciona una sensación de apertura y espacio. En claro contraste con los monumentales y vastos proyectos de construcción actualmente en curso en el centro de Tokio, Iwaoka crea una obra decente y de proporciones humanas.

e-mail: iwaoka@keyaki.cc.u-tokai.ac.jp Photos: Tatsuo Iwaoka Completion date: 2001

Section

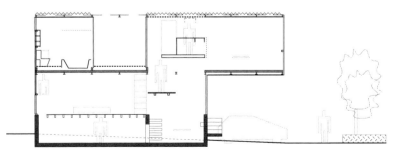

Bunkyo, a district famous for containing the prestigious University of Tokyo and many other educational institutions, also boasts the "Suzuki House", with its strikingly original facade. Its owner, Mr. Suzuki, is a renowned architecture and design critic. The building's design is the work of the studio of the architect Peter Wilson, an old friend of Mr. Suzuki and a former professor at AA School in London, well-known for projects like the Münster library. The household is completed by Mr. Suzuki's wife, an editor, their two children, and the family dog.

In Bunkyo, einem angesehenen Viertel von Tokio mit der berühmten Universität von Tokio und vielen weiteren akademischen Lehrzentren befindet sich das „Suzuki House" mit seiner originellen Fassade. Der Besitzer, Herr Suzuki, ist ein bekannter Architektur- und Design-Kritiker. Ein alter Freund von ihm, der Architekt Peter Wilson, ein ehemaliger Lehrer der „AA School" in London, und sein Studio, das ebenfalls bekannte Gebäude wie z. B. die Bibliothek von Münster realisiert hat, haben das Design seines Hauses entworfen. Der übrige Haushalt besteht aus der Ehefrau von Herrn Suzuki, einer Verlegerin, zwei Kindern und einem Hund.

Bunkyo, un district de Tokyo célèbre pour accueillir la prestigieuse Université de Tokyo et nombre d'autres institutions d'étude, est le quartier hébergeant la maison « Suzuki House », et sa façade originale et ostentatoire. Son propriétaire, M. Suzuki, est un critique d'architecture et de design de renom. La conception de l'édifice a été implémentée par l'architecte Peter Wilson, un ancien ami de M. Suzuki, précédemment professeur à l'AA School de Londres, et son étude, également connue pour des œuvres comme la bibliothèque Münster. Le foyer est complété par l'épouse de M. Suzuki, éditeur, leurs deux enfants et le chien.

Bunkyo, un célebre barrio de Tokio en donde tienen su sede la prestigiosa Universidad de Tokio y muchas otras instituciones académicas, es la zona en la que se halla la casa Suzuki con su original fachada. Su propietario, el señor Suzuki, es un conocido crítico de arquitectura y diseño. El diseño de la casa lo realizó un antiguo amigo suyo, el arquitecto Peter Wilson, antiguo profesor de la AA School de Londres, y su estudio, también responsable de edificios de renombre como la biblioteca de Münster. En la vivienda habitan también la esposa del señor Suzuki, editora, sus dos hijos y un perro.

Photos: Noriko Suzuki, Akira Suzuki (façade) Completion date: 1993

This house, with its striking C-shape marks on the facade, evoking an eye-testing card, serves as both an ophthalmologic clinic and a private residence, right in the heart of Tokyo's central Shibuya district. With the clinic located on the ground floor, the private areas of the house gradually reveal themselves over the course of the upper floors, with the living and dining rooms on the first floor and the private bedrooms on the second. Following a special request from the client, the architect Guen Bertheau-Suzuki placed a wild cherry tree on the terrace next to the living room, as a symbol of the spot. The oval window looking onto the semi-transparent terrace seems like a painting, and provides an emblematic urban touch.

Dieses Haus im Viertel von Shibuya direkt im Zentrum von Tokio zeigt einige eindrucksvolle Zeichen in C-Form an der rechten Seite seiner Fassade, die man als Augentest interpretieren könnte. Im Erdgeschoss befindet sich eine Augenklinik, im oberen Teil sind Privaträume, so dass man beim Hochgehen zuerst auf das Ess- und Wohnzimmer im ersten Stockwerk trifft und dann auf die Zimmer in der zweiten Etage. Als Sonderauftrag seines Kunden pflanzte der Architekt Guen Bertheau-Suzuki auf der Terrasse als Symbol des Ortes einen herrlichen Kirschbaum. Diese halbdurchsichtige Terrasse zusammen mit dem ovalen Fenster verleihen dem Komplex einen emblematischen urbanen Charakter - als wäre er ein Bild.

Cette demeure, avec ses marques « C », si impressionnantes sur sa façade avant, révèle vaguement une sorte test de vision et abrite une clinique ophtalmologique ainsi qu'une résidence. Elle est située au cœur de Shibuya, la circonscription centrale de Tokyo. La clinique étant au rez-de-chaussée, les zones privées apparaissent graduellement en franchissant les niveaux de l'immeuble, le séjour et la salle à manger au premier et les chambres au second. Sur demande spéciale du client, l'architecte Bertheau-Suzuki a placé un cerisier sauvage sur la terrasse, à côté du séjour, en symbole de la maison. La fenêtre elliptique ouverte et sa terrasse semi-transparente présentent, comme une peinture, un air urbain emblématique.

Esta casa, que muestra unos impresionantes signos en forma de C en la parte derecha de su fachada, que bien podrían interpretarse como la representación de un examen ocular, se halla situada en el barrio de Shibuya, en pleno centro de Tokio. El edificio hace a la vez las funciones de clínica oftalmológica, situada en su planta baja, y de residencia privada en su parte superior, de modo que a medida que se va ascendiendo por el inmueble se accede al comedor y salón situados en el primer piso o a las habitaciones del segundo. Por encargo especial de su cliente, el arquitecto Guen Bertheau-Suzuki colocó un precioso cerezo en la terraza, como símbolo del lugar. Dicha terraza semitransparente junto con la ventana oval abierta confieren al conjunto, como si de un cuadro de tratara, un carácter emblemático y urbano.

e-mail: gbs@attglobal.net Photos: Nacása & Partners Completion date: 1999

斎 田 医 院

This surgical clinic and private house, with the cross standing out conspicuously on the facade, was built near a train station in Yokohama, a city absorbed by conurbation of Greater Tokyo. On its roof, the house sports nothing less than a basketball court, resembling a huge bird cage; here, the children play, the owner sunbathes in his lunch break and the whole family regularly eat their meals, with dishes brought up from the first to the fifth floor by a tiny, purpose-built elevator. As the building is visually striking, and therefore attracts the attention of the train commuters who pass by, the clinic attracts an ever-increasing number of patients.

Dieses Haus in der Nähe eines Bahnhofes in Yokohama, das zum Siedlungsgebiet von Tokio gehört, ist zugleich Arztpraxis und Privatwohnung und fällt durch das eindrucksvolle Kreuz an seiner Fassade auf. Auf dem Dach dieses Gebäudes erhebt sich wie ein riesiger Vogelkäfig nichts Geringeres als ein Basketballplatz. Dort spielen die Kinder, man findet Entspannung, der Eigentümer sonnt sich während der Mittagspause, die ganze Familie isst dort regelmäßig im Freien und benutzt ihn als Bühne. Gut sichtbar für die Zugreisenden der Umgebung hat die Anzahl der Patienten der Privatpraxis in spektakulärem Maße zugenommen.

Cette clinique chirurgicale et résidence privée, avec sa croix omniprésente en façade, a été construite près d'une station de train à Yokohama, une ville de la conurbation du Grand Tokyo. Sur son toit, la demeure arbore un terrain de basket-ball, telle une gigantesque volière, où les enfants peuvent s'amuser, les propriétaires se baigner de soleil et toute la famille prendre ses repas régulièrement, les plats montant du premier au cinquième par un petit monte-plats installé à cet effet. La maison étant particulièrement visible, et attirant conséquemment l'attention des voyageurs journaliers, le nombre des patients contactant la clinique a singulièrement augmenté.

Esta casa, que destaca por la gran cruz de su fachada, ubicada cerca de una estación de tren en Yokohama, ciudad unida a la gran conurbación de Tokio, hace las funciones de consultorio clínico y de casa particular. El edificio destaca por la presencia en lo alto de su tejado de una notoria pista de baloncesto, de parecido similar a una gran jaula de pájaros. Espacio multifuncional utilizado por los hijos para jugar, de relax en donde el propietario acostumbra a tomar el sol durante su descanso del mediodía, es utilizado regularmente como comedor al aire libre para toda la familia. Fácilmente visible por los pasajeros de los trenes que circulan por sus inmediaciones, su consulta privada ha visto incrementado su número de pacientes de forma espectacular.

e-mail: gbs@attglobal.net Photos: Nacása & Partners Completion date: 1998

This new house, built in the city of Hasuda, an area in the Saitama region where open fields and farms can still be seen, has become a local landmark. Put up on an oddly shaped piece of land, the architect made the most of this irregularity by building the house right to the edges of the plot, in order to gain more space for its inner garden and secure the privacy of its occupants. The resulting structure, which faces a number of directions, endows each of its rooms with pleasant views and abundant sunshine. The family living in this house still marvels at the sight of the moon's luminous intensity pouring through their windows.

Dieses Haus in der Stadt Hasuda, einem Teil der Präfektur von Saitama, wo Felder und Bauernhöfe noch überleben konnten, wurde zu einem Meilenstein in der Landschaft dieser Stadt. Der Architekt behob die Mängel des Grundstückes indem er das Gebäude längs der Grenzlinien errichtete und so genügend Raum für einen Innengarten gewann und gleichzeitig die Intimität seiner Bewohner schützen konnte. Infolge der nach verschiedenen Richtungen hin ausgerichteten Struktur genießt man in allen Räumen außergewöhnliche Ausblicke und reichlich Tageslicht. Die Familie in diesem Haus erfreut sich außerdem noch an der intensiven Leuchtkraft des Mondes, wenn seine Strahlen durch die Fenster einfallen.

Cette nouvelle maison, construite à Hasuda, une ville de la préfecture de Saitama riche en champs ouverts et en fermes, est devenue une curiosité du paysage municipal. Érigée sur une parcelle déformée, l'architecte a tiré le meilleur parti de ses irrégularités en construisant le long de la ligne de démarcation du terrain, afin de libérer un espace suffisant pour le jardin intérieur et préserver la vie privée de ses occupants. La structure résultante, orientée selon diverses directions, offre de belles vues et fait abonder le soleil dans chaque pièce. La famille y vivant s'étonne encore à l'apparition d'une lune à l'intensité lumineuse, filtrant par les fenêtres.

Esta casa construida en la ciudad de Hasuda, una parte de la prefectura de Saitama que con sus campos y sus granjas todavía conserva un cierto aire campestre, se ha convertido en un punto destacado del paisaje de dicha ciudad. El arquitecto suplió las deficiencias en la configuración del solar levantando el edificio a lo largo de la línea de demarcación de su perímetro, lo cual le permitió ganar suficiente espacio para crear un jardín interior y asegurar también la intimidad de sus ocupantes. Como resultado de una estructura orientada en diferentes direcciones, todas las estancias de la casa gozan de excelentes vistas y abundante luz solar. La familia que habita esta casa continúa deleitándose con la magnífica visión de la intensidad de los rayos lunares penetrando por sus amplios ventanales.

Kanematsu House ● Guen Bertheau-Suzuki e-mail: gbs@attglobal.net Photos: Nacása & Partners Completion date: 1995

The symbolic series of circles constitutes the distinctive feature of the Ozawa House. Although the house contains several rooms with tatami floors, it seems to have a somewhat European air. The building was designed by the architect Guen Bertheau-Suzuki, born in Paris to a French mother and a Japanese father. It is home to a young married couple with children living on the first floor, and to the husband's mother on the second. So, there are two households, each with their respective entrance, living room and kitchen. A number of high circular windows are dotted around the building. Although they do not really provide any views of the exterior, they are enough to reassure each component of the family that the other one is always there.

Die symbolischen Kreiskomplexe sind das Auffallendste am Haus Ozawa. Selbst wenn verschiedene Zimmer mit Tatami-Boden ausgelegt sind, kann eine gewisse europäische Atmosphäre nicht verleugnet werden. Dieses Werk wurde von dem in Paris als Sohn eines japanischen Vaters und einer französischen Mutter geborenen Architekten Guen Bertheau-Suzuki entworfen. Das Haus beherbergt im ersten Stockwerk ein junges Ehepaar mit Kindern und in der zweiten Etage die Mutter des Ehemannes. Es handelt sich praktisch um zwei Häuser, um zwei Familien, mit getrenntem Eingang, Wohnzimmer und Küche. Hier und dort sind hoch angebrachte, runde Fenster eingelassen, die dazu beitragen, dass jede Familie die Anwesenheit der anderen bemerkt.

Les séries symboliques de cercles représentent les caractéristiques distinctives de la maison Ozawa. Bien qu'abritant plusieurs pièces à tatamis, la maison affiche cependant une certaine ambiance européenne. L'architecte Guen Bertheau-Suzuki, né à Paris d'une mère française et d'un père japonais, a conçu la demeure. Le projet accueille un jeune couple marié et ses enfants, au premier étage, et la mère du père de famille au second. Coexistent ainsi deux foyers avec leurs propres entrée, séjour et cuisine. Ça et là sont positionnées en hauteur plusieurs grandes fenêtres circulaires. Bien que ne se prêtant pas à l'intrusion dans la vie privée, elles contribuent à donner à chaque foyer des indications sur la présence de l'autre.

El conjunto simbólico de círculos constituye la característica principal de la casa Ozawa. Aunque contiene varias habitaciones con suelo de tatami, hay en la misma un cierto aire y ambiente europeo. El arquitecto Guen Bertheau-Suzuki, nacido en París de padre japonés y madre francesa, diseñó esta obra. En el edificio viven un joven matrimonio con hijos en el primer piso y la madre del marido en el segundo. En la práctica se trata de dos casas, dos familias, con entrada, salón y cocina separadas. A través de las ventanas circulares situadas estratégicamente en espacios elevados, cada familia tiene conciencia de la existencia de la otra y viceversa.

e-mail: gbs@attglobal.net Photos: Nacása & Partners Completion date: 1995

This house, located on a plot of land measuring 7,212 square feet, lies right in the heart of Tokyo, in the Meguro district. Although some of the flats in this condominium are for rent, the photos here show the apartment of the building's owner, with its lovely interior sporting touches reminiscent of the 80s. The architect, after carefully investigating the owner's tastes and preferences, sketched out the distinctive designs of the ceiling in the breakfast room and on the frosted glass windows and specially made furniture, and then commissioned a professional artist the breakfast room ceiling fresco.

Dieses Haus auf einem Grundstück von 670 m² steht im Viertel von Meguro direkt im Zentrum der Hauptstadt Tokio. Obwohl der größte Teil aus Mietwohnungen besteht, zeigen die Fotos das vom Eigentümer des Gebäudes bewohnte Apartment mit seiner luxuriösen Inneneinrichtung, die an die Extravaganz der achtziger Jahre erinnert. Nachdem sich der Architekt über den Geschmack und die Vorlieben des Eigentümers informiert hatte, entwarf er die ganz besondere Gestaltung der Decke im Frühstücksraum, des geschliffenen Glases der Fenster und des maßgefertigten Mobiliars und beauftragte später einen Künstler und Maler mit dem größten Teil der Ausführung der Arbeiten.

Sur un site de 670 m², cette maison se trouve au cœur de Tokyo, dans la circonscription de Meguro. Bien que certains des appartements de la copropriété soient à louer, les photos correspondent à celui du propriétaire de l'immeuble, aux superbes intérieurs marqués d'une touche de réminiscence des années 80. Ayant pris la mesure des goûts et préférences du propriétaire, puis ébauché et donné les grandes lignes caractéristiques et distinctives du plafond de la salle de petit-déjeuner, des fenêtres dépolies et du mobilier créé sur commande, l'architecte a engagé un artiste-peintre professionnel pour la frésque du plafond de la salle de petit déjeuner.

Esta casa, ubicada en una parcela de 670 m², se halla situada en el barrio de Meguro, en pleno centro de Tokio capital. Aunque la mayor parte del edificio está destinada a apartamentos de alquiler, las fotografías corresponden al apartamento habitado por el propietario del edificio, con un interiorismo lujoso que evoca a la extravagancia de los años ochenta. Este caso también se da en esta vivienda. El arquitecto, una vez al tanto de los gustos y preferencias del propietario de la casa, dibujó y esbozó las particulares características del techo de la sala de desayuno, del cristal esmerilado de las ventanas y del mobiliario hecho a medida. Posteriormente encargó la mayor parte de la realización del trabajo a un artista.

e-mail: gbs@attglobal.net Photos: Nacása & Partners Completion date: 1995

This building is located in Azabu, an area in central Tokyo popular with embassies and international schools. Within walking distance of the famous night-time hotspots of Roppongi and the perennially popular Azabu Juban shopping district, this is a convenient and attractive part of the city in which to live. In this Millenium Tower, a restaurants occupies the space between the basement and the second floor. The third and fourth floors are given over a manicure salon, while the remaining four floors are used for residential purposes, with four rented apartments. Despite their limited size of around 540 square feet, each apartment has 16-foot high ceilings and wide windows, allowing their occupants to enjoy a sense of spaciousness.

Dieses Gebäude steht im Zentrum von Tokio, in Azabu, einer Gegend mit einer großen Konzentration von Botschaften und internationalen Schulen. Nur wenige Schritte entfernt vom bekannten Mekka des Nachtlebens, Roppongi, und in der Nähe des alten und populären Einkaufszentrums Azabu Juban, ist dies ein Platz, an dem es sich angenehm leben lässt. Im Millenium-Tower befindet sich zwischen dem Erdgeschoss und der zweiten Etage ein Restaurant. Die dritte und vierte Etage sind einem „Nail Salon" vorbehalten, während in den letzten Etagen bis zum achten Stockwerk vier 50m^2 große Apartments untergebracht sind, deren relativ geringe Fläche jedoch durch fünf Meter hohe Decken und weite fröhliche Fenster ausgeglichen wird.

L'immeuble se trouve dans un quartier central de Tokyo, Azabu, point de convergence de nombre d'ambassades et écoles internationales. À quelques minutes de Roppongi, la célèbre Mecque de la vie nocturne, et du quartier des boutiques d'Azabu Juban, populaire depuis des temps immémoriaux, cette partie de la ville offre une vie facile et plaisante. Dans cette tour du Millenium, un restaurant occupe la zone du rez-de-chaussée au deuxième. Les troisième et quatrième niveaux appartiennent à un salon de manucure, les quatre étages restants, du cinquième au huitième, accueillant au total quatre logements en location. Malgré leur petitesse, quelque 50 mètres carrés, chaque appartement offre calme et détente grâce à des baies vitrées de cinq mètres de large et de haut.

Este edificio se halla situado en la zona de Azabu, lugar donde hay una gran concentración de embajadas y escuelas internacionales. A poca distancia del área de Roppongi, famosa por su animada vida nocturna, y del antiguo y popular distrito comercial de Azabu Juban, es una parte de la ciudad bien situada y cómoda para vivir. En el interior de la torre Millenium, un restaurante ocupa el espacio entre el sótano y el segundo piso, los pisos tercero y cuarto contienen un gran "nail salon" y las últimas cuatro plantas, de la quinta a la octava, están reservadas como espacio para vivienda, dando cabida a cuatro apartamentos de 50 m^2. Su relativamente reducido tamaño se ve compensado por techos de cinco metros de altura y por amplios y alegres ventanales.

e-mail: gbs@atglobal.net Photos: Nacása & Partners Completion date: 2000

This triangular house was built on a hill in the Hachioji area, on the outskirts of western Tokyo. Its distinctive lines suggest a rocket about to be launched into space, but a closer inspection reveals interiors that are extremely functional and comfortable. The design was drawn up by the German-born architect Andrea Held for the Hikone architectural firm; this was founded in 1990 by Held and her husband, Hikone, after they met working together in Arata Isozaki's studio. Since then, they have realized a wide variety of buildings, particularly outstanding housing projects that have been highly praised by both the media and specialty magazines.

In den Außenbezirken von Tokio finden wir auf einem kleinen Hügel von Hachioji im Westen der Hauptstadt dieses lustige, dreieckige Haus, das aussieht wie eine Rakete, die gleich ins Weltall geschossen wird. Sobald wir jedoch eintreten, sehen wir uns einer angenehmen, funktionellen und komfortablen Einrichtung gegenüber. Das Design stammt von der deutschen Architektin Andrea Held und ihrem Studio, das sie und ihr Mann Hikone im Jahr 1990 eröffneten, nachdem sie vorher zusammen im Atelier von Arata Isozaki gearbeitet hatten. Seitdem haben sie vielerlei Projekte, vorwiegend jedoch Häuser entworfen, die großen Anklang in Fachkreisen und in Fachzeitschriften fanden.

À la périphérie ouest de Tokyo, cette maison triangulaire se dresse sur une colline de la zone de Hachioji. Son apparence quelque peu amusante lui donne l'air d'une fusée prête pour un lancement dans l'espace. Pourtant, un examen plus approfondi permet de découvrir ses intérieurs extrêmement fonctionnels et confortables. Le design est dû à l'architecte Andrea Held, née allemande, et à l'étude d'architecte Hikone, en activité depuis 1990, lorsque, avec Hikone, son mari, elle créa l'étude après qu'ils aient fait connaissance à l'atelier d'Arata Isozaki. Depuis lors, ils ont collectionné les œuvres les plus diverses, des projets de logement particulièrement exceptionnels attirant l'attention des médias professionnels et des revues spécialisées.

En las afueras de Tokio, construida sobre una pequeña colina de Hachioji, en la parte oeste de la capital, encontramos esta divertida casa de estructura triangular, cuyas formas bien podrían recordarnos a un cohete a la espera de ser lanzado al espacio. No obstante, al adentrarnos en ella pronto descubrimos un interiorismo agradable, funcional y confortable. Su diseño ha sido realizado por la arquitecta alemana Andrea Held y su estudio, el cual viene operando desde 1990, año en que ella y su marido, Hikone, decidieron abrirlo después de haber trabajado ambos en el taller de arquitectura de Arata Isozaki. Desde entonces han realizado todo tipo de obras, en particular proyectos de casas que han tenido mucha resonancia entre los medios de comunicación y las revistas especializadas del sector.

e-mail: aha004@aol.com Photos: Nacása & Partners Completion date: 2002

Section

This new house was built, in part, to satisfy the growing demands on space made by its owners' stunning book collection. Eventually this couple – formed by a journalist and an editorial assistant – decided to build this new house in Machida. The architects respected the atmosphere of the building's surroundings by incorporating features like a red roof, red window frames and a stone-paved parking lot. In the basement, there is a private library which contains over ten thousand books, as if the whole structure of the building was founded on this huge collection; it is certainly the case that this vast treasure-trove has marked the life of the occupants living above.

Dieses Haus wurde teilweise deswegen gebaut, weil seine Eigentümer, ein mit einer Redakteurin verheirateter Journalist, einfach nicht mehr wussten, wo sie ihre eindrucksvolle Büchersammlung unterbringen sollten, die ihnen keinen Platz mehr übrig ließ. Sie entschieden sich für den Bau dieses neuen Gebäudes in Machida. Dem Charakter der Umgebung wird von den Architekten unter anderem durch ein rotes Dach, roten Fensterrahmen und einem mit Feldsteinen gepflasterten Parkplatz Rechnung getragen. Im Kellergeschoss befindet sich die Bibliothek des Ehepaares mit über zehntausend Bänden. Es scheint fast so, als ob das Fundament der Gebäudestruktur auf dieser beeindruckenden Büchersammlung ruhe.

Cette nouvelle maison est née en partie parce que ses propriétaires, un couple journaliste-éditeur, étaient désemparés face à la quantité d'espace dévorée par leur collection de livres. Ils ont fini par décider de construire cette nouvelle demeure, dans Machida, à Tokyo. Les architectes ont conçu l'immeuble en respectant l'atmosphère du cadre, incorporant ainsi un toit rouge, des embrasures de fenêtre rouges et un parking pavé. Le sous-sol accueille une bibliothèque privée de plus de dix mille livres. La structure entière de l'édifice semble reposer sur cette vaste collection. Celle-ci contribue certainement à donner forme à la vie de ses habitants.

Esta casa se construyó en parte porque sus propietarios, un matrimonio compuesto por un periodista y una editora, estaban constantemente devanándose los sesos sobre qué hacer con la impresionante colección de libros que les robaba tanto espacio. Finalmente optaron por construir este nuevo edificio en Machida, en donde los arquitectos, respetando el estilo ya existente en esta zona, incorporan a su estructura elementos como un tejado y marcos de ventanas en color rojo, así como un parking pavimentado en piedra. El sótano contiene la biblioteca, con un número de volumenes superior a diez mil. Es casi como si toda la estructura del edificio tuviera como cimientos esta impresionante colección de libros, algo que ciertamente condiciona la vida de sus moradores.

e-mail: **aha004@aol.com** Photos: **Nobuaki Nakagawa** Completion date: **2001**

The entrance of this detached four-storied house located in Tokyo's Shibuya ward lies right in the middle of the two interconnected towers that form the structure of the building. Both husband and wife made their dreams come true by incorporating to the interior design of their house details like an open-air bath on the roof and a mosaic-tiled bathroom. The husband's study, a tatami room used as his private retreat, was built inside a section of the main bedroom adopting the structure of a small maisonette. The transformation of light and scenery experienced by the tenants when moving around indoors through the glass bridge is quite reinvigorating.

Der Eingang zu diesem vierstöckigen Haus im Viertel von Shibuya in Tokio befindet sich direkt in der Mitte der zwei miteinander verbundenen Türme, die die Struktur des Gebäudes bilden. Die Eigentümer sind ein Ehepaar, das hier seine Träume in Realität umsetzte, mit Elementen wie Mosaikkacheln im Bad oder einer Badewanne auf dem Dach. In einem Teil des Hauptschlafzimmers ist erhöht ein Studio mit Tatami-Fußboden eingerichtet worden, in das sich der Ehemann zurückziehen kann. Die Wandlung von Licht und Szene beim Gehen durch die Innenräume über die Kristallbrücke vermittelt das Gefühl von Vitalität.

L'entrée de cette maison indépendante de quatre étages de Shibuya, une circonscription de Tokyo, se situe juste entre deux tours interconnectées, formant la structure de l'édifice. Mari et femme ont donné vie à leurs rêves en intégrant au design intérieur de leur maison des détails tel un bain à ciel ouvert sur le toit et une salle de bain en mosaïques. L'atelier du mari, une salle de tatamis servant de refuge privé, a été construit dans une section de la chambre principale adoptant la forme d'une petite maisonnette. La transformation de la lumière et du paysage vécue par les habitants au gré de leurs déplacements dans la maison, dans le pont vitré, s'avère très stimulante.

La entrada a esta casa de cuatro pisos del barrio de Shibuya, en Tokio, se halla ubicada justo en medio de las dos torres interconectadas que conforman la estructura del edificio. El matrimonio propietario de la misma hizo realidad su sueño de incorporar al interiorismo de la vivienda detalles tales como una bañera al aire libre ubicada en el terrado, así como decorar el baño con diminutos azulejos tipo mosaico. En una parte del dormitorio principal, como si de un dúplex se tratara, encontramos el estudio-biblioteca, con suelo de tatami, utilizado por el marido como su particular refugio. El cambio en la luz y paisaje que experimentan los inquilinos al cruzar el interior de la casa a través del puente de cristal les proporciona sensaciones de vitalidad.

NAG ● Andrea Held

e-mail: aha004@aol.com Photos: Nacása & Partners Completion date: 2000

This house is set in Tokyo's Shinjuku district, where tradition rubs shoulders with spectacular high-rise buildings. It is situated at the end of a narrow alley-way, with part of its porch crossing the entire building, under the piloti, to reach the garden. This layout has proved attractive to the local children of the vicinity, who go across the porch to the garden, where they can play in freedom. All in all, it is a sociable household, made with ecologically friendly materials; its owner, a jazz musician, thrives on his personal recording studio in the basement, where he can sometimes be found jamming with his neighbors.

Dies ist die traditionelle Gegend des Viertels Shinjuku in Tokio, wo alte und neue Bauten sowie aufsehenerregende Wolkenkratzer miteinander kontrastieren. In diesem Haus in einer der engen Sträßchen durchquert ein Teil der Vorhalle unter dem Piloti das ganze Gebäude bis zum Garten. Diese Art von Struktur lädt die Kinder der Nachbarschaft dazu ein, das Gebäude zu betreten, durch die Vorhalle zu laufen und übermütig im Garten zu spielen. Bei diesem sympathischen Familienhaus wurden auch ökologische und gesundheitsfreundliche Materialien verwendet. Der Eigentümer, ein Jazz-Musiker, hat sein eigenes Studio im Kellergeschoss, wo er auch ab und zu die Nachbarn zum Jazzspielen einlädt.

Dans ce coin traditionnel de la circonscription Shinjuku de Tokyo, l'ancien entre en collision avec le nouveau symbolisé par les spectaculaires gratte-ciel de la cité. Dans cette maison, au bout d'une allée étroite, une partie du porche située sous des pilotis dépasse l'édifice pour entrer dans le jardin. Ce type de structure attire les enfants du voisinage, qui tentent d'envahir la maison pour galoper dans le jardin. Un lieu social et amical, intégrant des matériaux sains et respectueux de l'environnement, au cœur duquel son propriétaire, un musicien de jazz, jouit de son propre studio d'enregistrement en sous-sol où, parfois, il se lance dans des sessions de jazz avec ses voisins.

Estamos en una zona tradicional del barrio Shinjuku de Tokio, en donde lo viejo se enfrenta a los nuevos y espectaculares rascacielos de la zona. En esta casa ubicada en una de sus estrechas callejuelas una parte de su porche, situado debajo del piloti, atraviesa todo el edificio hasta el jardín. Este tipo de estructura invita a los niños del vecindario a entrar en el edificio cruzando el porche, y a correr por todo el jardín desenfadadamente. Dicha casa familiar sociable y simpática incluye en su estructura materiales ecológicos y sanos. Su propietario, un músico de jazz, posee su propio estudio de grabación en el sótano, lugar en el que a veces realiza sesiones de jazz con vecinos.

e-mail: aha004@aol.com Photos: Nacása & Partners Completion date: 1998

The architects satisfied their client's brief of a residential building that could reflect a contemporary version of a traditional and popular Japanese minka-style house. Simple, with no corridors, with adjoining quadrilateral rooms, the house features large eaves, a classical engawa terrace, a kitchen and a hearth right in the middle of the living room. In winter the whole family can sit and enjoy themselves by the fire, warming up sake and grilling fish. The house is occupied by a family of three, with the wife controlling her kimono-dyeing business from the studio on the upper floor.

Die Architekten erfüllten die Wünsche ihres Kunden und entwarfen dieses Gebäude als moderne Version des tradtionellen und volkstümlichen japanischen „Minka-Hauses". Einfach, ohne Gänge, mit viereckigen, aneinandergereihten Zimmern, fällt das Haus durch seinen großen Dachvorsprung auf. Des weiteren gehört dazu eine typisch japanische Galerie oder „Engawa", die Küche und ein offener Kamin mitten im Wohnzimmer, um den herum sich die Familie versammelt und Saké erwärmt oder Fisch grillt. In der Werkstatt im Obergeschoss führt die Ehefrau dieses Drei-Personen-Haushalts ihr Geschäft des Kimono-Färbens.

Les architectes ont donné vie aux souhaits de leur client en concevant un immeuble résidentiel reflétant une version contemporaine du style traditionnel et populaire de maison japonaise « Minka ». Simple, sans couloir, avec des pièces quadrilatérales adjacentes, la maison intègre de larges avant-toits, une véranda japonaise « Engawa » classique, une cuisine et un âtre au centre du séjour. En hiver, la famille peut s'asseoir et s'amuser autour du feu, réchauffant le saké et grillant le poisson. Au sein de ce foyer de trois personnes, l'épouse peut gérer son affaire de teinture de kimonos depuis l'atelier, à l'étage supérieur.

Los arquitectos diseñaron este edificio de forma que respondiera a las expectativas de su cliente de poder tener una versión actualizada de la tradicional y popular casa minka japonesa. Simple, sin pasillos, con habitaciones cuadrangulares contiguas, la casa destaca por el gran alero de su tejado e incluye una típica galería japonesa o engawa, cocina y un hogar de fuego situado en el centro del salón, alrededor del cual la familia se reúne para disfrutar, calentando sake y preparando pescado a la parrilla. La esposa de esta familia de tres personas dirige su negocio de tinte para kimonos desde el taller ubicado en la planta superior.

e-mail: aha004@aol.com Photos: Nacasa & Partners Completion date: 1995

This house is located in a densely built-up area in Tokyo's Ota district; its triangular roof is the consequence of the legal regulations imposed by the Tokyo authorities on new buildings. Its purpose is to avoid any obstacles to sunlight reaching the neighboring buildings. The architects considered it not as an imposition but more as an opportunity to create a challenging interior space. The interior design is distinguished by a mobile kitchen that evokes a stage setting, with a detachable counter that can be put into use during social gatherings and parties. The immaculate white expanses of the house's interiors express the owners' desire to restart their life from zero.

In der dicht besiedelten Gegend des Viertels Ota in Tokio wurde dieses Haus in Befolgung der gesetzlichen Vorschriften für Neubauten in Tokio mit einem dreieckigem Dach gebaut, um den benachbarten Gebäuden kein Licht wegzunehmen. Mehr als nur eine Auflage, bedeutete dies für die Architekten eine Herausforderung für die anregende Gestaltung der Inneneinrichtung. Besonders auffallend ist die Küche mit Szenenwechseln wie auf einer Theaterbühne. Bei Festen oder gesellschaftlichen Ereignissen kann ein Teil abgetrennt und in Theke und Bar umgewandelt werden. Der makellos weiße Innenanstrich reflektiert den Wunsch der Bewohner, ein neues Leben anzufangen.

Dans une zone de construction intense de la circonscription tokyoïte de Ota, le toit en triangle de cette demeure est la conséquence des normes imposées par les autorités de Tokyo aux nouveaux édifices. Il a pour objet d'éviter de cacher la lumière du soleil aux maisons avoisinantes. Pour les architectes, ce fut plus une occasion de créer un espace intérieur stimulant qu'une réelle imposition. La conception intérieure de la maison propose des traits distinctifs comme une cuisine mobile évoquant un décor de théâtre, avec un comptoir détachable utilisable lors des fêtes et réceptions. La blancheur immaculée des intérieurs affirme la volonté des propriétaires de commencer une nouvelle vie.

Ubicada en una zona densamente poblada de viviendas del barrio de Ota de Tokio, las autoridades metropolitanas de la ciudad hicieron valer las restricciones vigentes para este tipo de áreas tan pobladas, y con el fin de evitar que su construcción obstruyera la llegada de luz solar a las edificaciones vecinas, esta casa se construyó con un tejado en forma de triángulo. Para los arquitectos, más que una imposición se trató de una oportunidad de crear un interiorismo estimulante. De entre sus peculiaridades destaca la cocina, con un funcionamiento que recuerda a una tramoya para el cambio de un escenario teatral: una parte de la misma se puede separar y ser utilizada como barra-mostrador en fiestas o actos sociales. El blanco inmaculado de sus interiores representa el deseo de sus dueños de empezar una nueva vida.

e-mail: info@milligram.ne.jp Photos: Takeshi Taira Completion date: 2000

This building, built on a plot of around 3,230 square feet, provides space for two separate households; the ground floor is home to a couple in their sixties, while their son lives on the top floor with his wife and their one year old son. milligram studio designed this house with the aim of satisfying two different generations, with different lifestyles and rhythms, who nevertheless shared the same roof. They opted for loose and partial connections between the two homes, both externally and internally, while guaranteeing the privacy of both family units. One anecdote concerning the architectural office is that one of the partners, Mr Utsumi, won a competition for set designs for the English National Ballet while he was studying at the Royal College of Art in London.

In diesem Haus auf einem Grundstück von rund 300 m² wohnen zwei Familien. Im Erdgeschoss leben die Eltern des jungen Ehemannes, der zusammen mit seiner Frau und seinem einjährigen Sohn die obere Etage bewohnt. Das Studio milligram entwarf diese Wohnungen mit dem Ziel, zwei Generationen verschiedener Einstellung und mit verschiedenem Lebensrhythmus unter einem Dach gerecht zu werden. Dazu entschieden sich die Architekten sowohl auf externer als auch auf interner Ebene für eine lose Verbindung und wahrten dabei die private Atmosphäre beider Wohnungen. Noch ein Wort zu dem Design-Studio: Herr Utsumi gewann während seiner Studentenzeit auf dem Royal College of Art in London den Preis für „Set Design Competition to Design the English National Ballet".

Deux foyers différents habitent dans la maison construite sur cette parcelle de quelques 300 m². Au rez-de-chaussée, vivent les parents, encore dans leur soixantaine, du jeune mari qui avec son épouse et leur petit d'un an occupent l'étage supérieur. L'étude milligram a conçu cette demeure avec à l'esprit l'idée que deux générations différentes, avec des approches probablement différentes de la vie et des rythmes de vie différents, pourraient coexister sous un même toit. Ainsi, ils ont favorisé une connexion libre et modérée des deux foyers, extérieure et intérieure, tout en maintenant la vie privée des deux familles. Travaillant avec le cabinet, tout en étudiant Royal College of Art de Londres, M. Utsumi a remporté le « Concours de création de décor de l'English National Ballet ».

Dos familias habitan esta casa construida en una parcela de 300 m². En la planta baja residen los padres del joven marido, que habita la planta superior del inmueble junto a su esposa y un hijo de un año. El estudio diseñó esta vivienda pensando en las dos generaciones que cohabitarían en la misma con un enfoque y ritmo de vida distintos. Para ello, manteniendo la intimidad de ambas familias, los arquitectos optaron por un diseño que conectara con moderación los dos pisos de la vivienda, tanto a nivel interno como externo. En referencia al estudio de diseño, el señor Utsumi ganó durante su época de estudiante en el Royal College of Art de Londres un concurso de decoración para el English National Ballet.

e-mail: info@milligram.ne.jp Photos: Takeshi Taira Completion date: 2002

An industrial designer and a jewellery designer constitute the couple who live in this three-story house located in Tokyo's central Shinjuku area, and they have put a workshop on the first floor of the premises. The architects managed to make good use of the existing gap between the outer structural wall and the inner wall to create a storage space. To disguise this, they put up a variety of colorful and attractive nylon screens, easily changeable if the occupants house grow tired of them. All in all, the interior design has a kaleidoscopic visual impact. As followers of the trends in audiovisual equipment, the owners have installed a movable 100-inch screen in the ceiling of the living room.

In diesem dreistöckigen Haus in dem zentralen Stadtviertel Shinjuku in Tokio leben ein Industrie-Designer und eine Schmuck-Designerin. Die erste Etage dient als Werkstatt. Die Architekten wandelten den leeren Raum zwischen den Wänden der Außen- und Innenstruktur in ein Lager um. Zur Abdeckung verwendeten sie fröhliche Nylonplatten in verschiedenen Farben, die leicht ausgewechselt werden können, falls der Kunde ein anderes Design möchte. Die allgemeine Inneneinrichtung könnte man in gewisser Weise als kaleidoskopisch bezeichnen. Da die Bewohner Fans von audio-visuellen Geräten sind, haben sie an der Decke des Ess-Wohnzimmers einen 100 Zoll großen beweglichen Bildschirm installiert.

Un designer industriel et une créatrice en joaillerie habitent en couple cette maison de trois étages de Shinjuku, une zone centrale de Tokyo. Au premier niveau de l'immeuble, ils ont décidé d'installer leur atelier. L'architecte a su tirer parti de l'espace vide existant entre le mur structurel extérieur et la cloison intérieure en créant de vastes espaces de rangement. Pour les recouvrir, toutes sortes d'écrans de nylon gais et colorés ont été employés. Ils sont également simplement interchangeables si les habitants venaient à s'en lasser. La conception intérieure de l'ensemble est de nature kaléidoscopique. Les propriétaires appréciant l'audiovisuel, ils ont installé un écran mobile de 2,50 m au plafond du living.

La pareja que habita esta casa de tres pisos, situada en el céntrico barrio de Shinjuku, está formada por un diseñador industrial y una diseñadora de joyas. El primer piso del inmueble es utilizado como taller de trabajo. Los arquitectos aprovecharon el vacío existente entre las paredes de estructura externa e interna para crear un espacio para ser usado como depósito o almacén. Para recubrir el mismo, aplicaron una serie de pantallas de nylon de colores variados y agradables a la vista. Éstas son fácilmente renovables en caso que el cliente se canse de su diseño. Como resultado, el interiorismo general de la casa podría en cierto modo definirse como de caleidoscopio. Los propietarios de la casa, como buenos amantes de los aparatos audiovisuales, se han hecho instalar una pantalla móvil de 100 pulgadas en el techo del salón.

Inner Skin House ● milligram Studio

e-mail: info@milligram.ne.jp Photos: Takeshi Taira Completion date: 2001

A former office building in a back alley in Shibuya, central Tokyo, built up in the 60s but long since fallen into disrepair, was regenerated thanks to an all-embracing refurbishment. The owners, a young professional married couple – the husband works for a large advertising agency and the wife used to be a model – bought and completely renovated this house. On the ground floor, the wife now runs her own business, the Fujiyama bar. The couple's living quarters are on the remaining two floors above. This is a positive example of the on-going trend to adapt to the existing environment and enhance the urban landscape through the regeneration and recovery of old buildings.

In einer Gasse im Zentrum von Tokio wurde dieses alte und sehr vernachlässigte Büro-Gebäude aus den sechziger Jahren von Grund auf renoviert. Die Eigentümer, ein junges Paar, der Ehemann arbeitet als Führungskraft bei einer bekannten Werbeagentur, die Ehefrau ist ein ehemaliges Modell, beauftragten das Architektur-Studio milligram mit der kompletten Sanierung des Gebäudes. Im Erdgeschoss betreibt die Ehefrau ihre Bar Fujiyama. In den beiden oberen Etagen liegen die Wohnräume des Paares. Dies ist ein interessantes Beispiel für die wachsende Tendenz des modernen Tokio, die Anpassung an die Umwelt zu optimieren und durch die Sanierung alter Gebäude das Stadtbild zu erhalten.

Dans une ruelle de Shibuya, au centre de Tokyo, cet ancien immeuble de bureaux des années 60 qui tombait en ruines a été rendu à la vie grâce une rénovation de fond en comble. Les propriétaires, un couple de jeunes professionnels, le mari travaillant pour une grande agence de publicité et l'épouse ancienne modèle, ont acquis et complètement réformé cette maison. Au rez-de-chaussée, l'épouse tient sa nouvelle affaire, le bar Fujiyama. Leur espace privé occupe les deux étages supérieurs restants. Celui-ci est un exemple de la tendance actuelle visant à mieux adapter l'environnement existant et recherchant l'amélioration du paysage urbain grâce à la régénération et à la récupération d'anciens immeubles.

En una callejuela de Shibuya, en el centro de Tokio, se ha recuperado, mediante una profunda renovación, este antiguo edificio de oficinas construido a principios de los sesenta. Sus propietarios, un joven matrimonio compuesto por un ejecutivo de una importante agencia de publicidad y por una antigua modelo, después de adquirir el inmueble, encargaron al estudio de arquitectura milligram la total remodelación del mismo. En la planta baja, la esposa se ocupa de la dirección de su propio negocio, el bar Fujiyama. En las dos plantas superiores se encuentran las dependencias dedicadas a vivienda particular de la pareja. He aquí un buen ejemplo de la creciente tendencia existente en el Tokio actual y que consiste en una mejora de la adaptación al medio ambiente así como de la conservación del paisaje urbano a través de la recuperación de edificios antiguos.

e-mail: info@milligram.ne.jp Photos: Takeshi Taira / Kozaburo Sakamoto Completion date: 2001

This is the private home of the architect who designed the house, located in a residential part of Tokyo's Setagaya district. In this project, the architect went to great lengths to ensure the flexibility of its interior space. So, the main bedroom and the children's room are divided only by partitions, which, like the light furniture, is easily removable should the need arise to create one large spacious area. The building structure and the foundations, which incorporate thick planks, are resistant to earthquakes, as well as been efficiently insulated from noise and fire. The house incorporates an original, circular stone-carved bath.

In diesem Haus in der Wohngegend des Viertels Setagaya in Tokio lebt der Architekt, der es entwarf. Bei diesem Projekt legte der Designer besonderen Nachdruck auf die flexible Innengestaltung. Daher wurden zum Beispiel das Elternschlafzimmer und das Kinderzimmer nur durch Zwischenwände getrennt, die man im Bedarfsfall, zusammen mit dem beweglichen Mobiliar, entfernen kann, um einen offenen und einzigen Raum zu erhalten. Die Struktur und das Fundament des Gebäudes bestehen aus dicken, erdbebenfesten Holzplatten, die geräuschisoliert und feuerfest sind. Erwähnenswert ist das originelle, runde, in Stein gehauene Badewanne.

C'est la demeure personnelle de l'architecte qui l'a conçue, située dans une aire résidentielle du district tokyoïte de Setagaya. Pour ce projet, l'architecte attache une grande importance à garantir la flexibilité de l'espace. À cet effet, la chambre principale et celle des enfants sont séparées uniquement par des partitions, aisément amovibles le long du mobilier de rangement pour devenir, le cas échéant, un espace vaste et ample. La structure et les fondations, en planches épaisses, sont résistantes aux séismes et efficacement protégées contre le son et le feu. La maison incorpore un original bain circulaire, creusé dans la pierre.

Esta casa, ubicada en una zona residencial del barrio Setagaya de Tokio, es la residencia del mismo arquitecto que la diseñó. Para este proyecto, su diseñador confiere especial importancia a la capacidad de aportar flexibilidad a sus interiores. Con esta finalidad, habitaciones como el dormitorio principal y el de los niños están separadas sólo por tabiques, los cuales, junto al mobiliario móvil, se pueden suprimir para crear un amplio espacio abierto y único. El edificio, cuya estructura y cimientos están formados por tablas de madera, está construido para resistir movimientos sísmicos. Su estructura también es aislante al paso del ruido y contra incendios. La vivienda incluye también un original baño, de forma circular, tallado en piedra.

Zig Zag House ● Nobuaki Furuya / Studio Nasca

e-mail: nasca@studio-nasca.com Photos: Mitsuo Matsuoka Completion date: 2001

This is a three-level apartment situated inside a modern, exposed-concrete house in Tokyo's Shibuya district. The first level is a sort of semi-basement with a small courtyard surrounded on all sides by exposed concrete. The second floor is the site of the main entrance. On the third floor, the second from the street, a slanted 15-foot ceiling is the main feature – a rarity in a city like Tokyo, where space is a precious commodity. The apartment was meant to be a pied-a-terre revolving around a collection of modern prints and paintings. Although the majority of the works are by Japanese artists, there are some European pieces and a notable Liechtenstein triptych.

Dieses dreistöckige Apartment befindet sich in einem modernen Gebäude aus Sichtbeton im Viertel Shibuya in Tokio. Auf der ersten Ebene finden wir eine Art Halb-Souterrain mit einem kleinen Hof, umgeben von Wänden aus Sichtbeton. Auf der zweiten Ebene fällt der Haupteingang ins Auge. Auf der dritten Ebene (der zweiten Etage in Bezug auf das Straßenniveau) besteht die Hauptattraktion in einem geneigten, 4,5 Meter hohen Dach, in einer Stadt mit so wenig Platz wie Tokio eine wirkliche Seltenheit. Dieses Apartment war als zweiter Wohnsitz gedacht, um moderne Drucke und Gemälde unterzubringen. Obwohl die meisten Bilder von japanischen Künstlern stammen, sind auch einige europäische Künstler vertreten sowie ein einmaliges Triptychon von Liechtenstein.

Cet appartement de trois niveaux est situé au sein d'une maison de béton, ouverte et moderne, de Shibuya, une circonscription tokyoïte. Le premier est une sorte de semi-sous-sol doté d'un patio entouré de béton nu. Le deuxième étage accueille la porte d'entrée. Le plafond fendu à 4,5 m constitue le principal attribut du troisième (le second étage depuis la rue). Plutôt étrange en regard de la valeur de l'espace dans une cité comme Tokyo. L'appartement devait censément servir de pied-à-terre, organisé autour d'une collection d'estampes et de peintures. La plupart des œuvres revient à des artistes japonais, mais l'on remarque certaines pièces européennes notamment un triptyque du Liechtenstein.

Este es un apartamento a tres niveles que se halla en un moderno edificio de hormigón a la vista situado en el barrio de Shibuya de Tokio. En el primer nivel encontramos una especie de semisótano en el que hay un pequeño patio rodeado por paredes de hormigón a la vista. En el segundo nivel destaca la puerta principal de entrada. El tercero (segundo desde el exterior), presenta como principal atributo un techo inclinado de 4,5 metros de altura, rara característica en una ciudad como Tokio en donde el espacio es un bien tan escaso. Este apartamento hace las funciones de segunda residencia para albergar modernas colecciones de grabados y pinturas. Aunque la mayoría de las obras son de artistas japoneses, hay también algunas piezas europeas y un singular tríptico de Liechtenstein.

e-mail: **mail@dasic.com** Photos: **Peter Cook** Completion date: **1997**

A married couple still in their 20's decided to refurbish the interior of the uniform and standard prefabricated house they had purchased earlier on. They commission its remodelling to Love the Life design studio, principally known in the shop design sector. They carried out the necessary reforms that enabled its dwellers to feel the living space more as their own, rather than a mass produced standard house. By employing dark brown wooden materials, pretended to avoid, on the one hand, the glossy and glittering artificial and economic effective materials used in the decoration of uniformly fabricated houses, while, on the other, trying to express a certain come-back to the old nostalgic concepts of the decoration prevalent during the 60's.

Ein junges Ehepaar beschloss, die Innenräume ihres zuvor gekauften Fertighauses zu renovieren. Sie beauftragten das Design-Studio Love the Life mit der Renovierung der Inneneinrichtung. Die Designer unternahmen die erforderlichen Umbauten, wobei sie so weit wie möglich die dekorative Unpersönlichkeit der in Serie hergestellten Fertighäuser verbannten und es so den Bewohnern ermöglichten, sich als die Herren der Räumlichkeiten zu fühlen. Sie verwendeten dunkelbraunes Holz und versuchten, die synthetischen glänzenden Materialien, die normalerweise in der Dekoration von Fertighäusern vorherrschen, zu unterdrücken. Damit wurde auch eine nostalgische Rückkehr zu den Dekorationskonzepten der sechziger Jahre beabsichtigt.

Un jeune couple décida de rénover l'intérieur de la maison préfabriquée qu'il venait d'acheter. Ils chargèrent le studio de décoration Love the Life de s'occuper de l'agencement et de la rénovation de l'intérieur. Le designer entreprit les transformations en essayant de changer les points impersonnels que les maisons préfabriquées et de série ont en soit, afin de procurer aux nouveaux habitants l'impression d'être les maîtres des lieux. Ils emploient de bois foncé, essayant de cette façon de masquer autant que possible les matériaux synthétiques et brillants, employés généralement dans la construction de maisons préfabriquées. Un retour nostalgique aux conceptes décoratifs des années soixantes fût également obtenu de cette manière.

Un joven matrimonio decidió rehacer el interiorismo de la casa prefabricada que había adquirido con anterioridad. Encargaron al estudio de diseño Love the Life la renovación de su interior. Los diseñadores realizaron las necesarias reformas que permitieran a sus moradores sentirse más dueños del espacio que habitaban, desterrando en lo posible la impersonalidad que refleja la decoración de toda casa prefabricada en serie. Apostó por la incorporación de madera en color marrón oscuro a su proyecto, de tal modo que les permitiera apartarse del uso de materiales artificiales brillantes aplicados normalmente en la decoración de casas prefabricadas. Con ello pretenden también reivindicar una vuelta, no exenta de nostalgia, a los conceptos prevalentes en la decoración de los años sesenta.

e-mail: info@lovethelife.org Photos: Seikoh Fukuma Completion date: 2002

The married couple that makes up the design studio Love the Life" moved into this small store which they now use as a living and working space. Despite being located in Deenchofu, in Tokyo's Ota district, famous for being an exclusive residential district, the house is situated in a rundown but fascinating shopping street reminiscent of the 1960s. This couple chose a lifestyle that permitted them to take full advantage of living in a small and close community; they committed themselves enthusiastically to the area's everday life and to brightening it up. Although the premises may be small, they astutely make the most of them by using the space as a store or a small gallery. It could be described as an experimental zone.

Das Ehepaar, das das Design-Studio Love the Life führt, zog in diesen kleinen Laden um, der nun als Wohnung und als Arbeitsplatz dient. Obwohl der Laden in Deenchofu, im Viertel Ota von Tokio liegt, das durch seine Exklusivität berühmt wurde, steht das Haus in einem der wenigen Ortsteile mit einer etwas dekadenten aber sehr interessanten Geschäftsstraße, die an die sechziger Jahre erinnert. Das Paar nimmt an dem Leben im Vorort teil und integriert sich begeistert und mit großer Vitalität in die nachbarschaftlichen Verpflichtungen. Trotz der reduzierten Dimensionen des Gebäudes haben sie mit Geschick alle Möglichkeiten genutzt und verwenden die Räume teils als Laden, teils auch als kleine Kunstgalerie. Man könnte es als ein Experimentierfeld beschreiben.

Le couple marié formant le studio de création Love the Life a emménagé dans ce petit magasin, site de travail et lieu de vie. Bien que située à Deenchofu, un quartier de la circonscription tokyoïte de Ota célèbre pour son caractère exclusivement résidentiel, la maison appartient à une zone accueillant une rue de magasin, aux réminiscences années 60, décadente mais intéressante. Ce couple a choisit un style de vie leur laissant profiter pleinement des avantages d'une petite communauté, se dévouant avec enthousiasme à la vie quotidienne de la ville et l'illuminant. La maison peut sembler petite mais son espace est parfaitement exploité, se transformant en magasin ou en galerie. Une sorte de cadre expérimental en somme.

El matrimonio que forma el estudio de diseño Love the Life se trasladó a esta pequeña tienda para utilizarla como lugar de trabajo y vivienda. A pesar de estar situada en Deenchofu, en el barrio de Ota, una zona de Tokio famosa por sus exclusivos barrios residenciales, la casa está en una de las pocas áreas del barrio que aún abriga una decadente pero entrañable calle comercial que nos permite volver a los años sesenta. La pareja optó por llevar una vida de barrio, comprometiéndose de forma entusiasta con el devenir del vecindario y aportando vitalidad al mismo. Podría bien describirse como un área experimental.

e-mail: info@lovethelife.org Photos: Susumu Koshimizu Completion date: 2001

Floor Plans

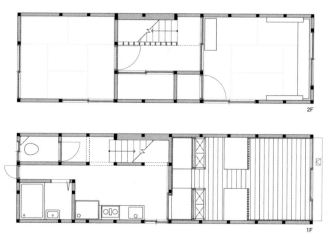

2F

1F

Section

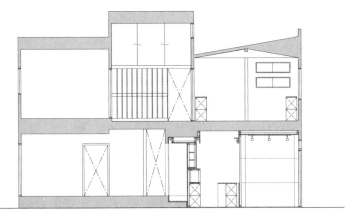

This house is located in the old downtown Tokyo area of Kanda, famous for its large number of old bookshops and containing the offices of many publishing companies. The owner of this apartment, once a musician, decided to reform the apartment to his own particular taste, after inheriting a printing company located in the same building. At night the space transforms into an informal jazz-bar type of venue where the owner socializes with his friends. His daughter's tiny room features delightful wallpaper with heart-shaped motifs and a hanging clock with the "Hello Kitty" cartoon character.

Dieses Haus steht in Kanda, dem alten Viertel von Tokio, bekannt für seine zahllosen alten Büchereien und als Sitz vieler Verlagsfirmen. Nachdem der Eigentümer die Familiendruckerei im gleichen Gebäude geerbt hatte, entschied er, dieses Apartment umzubauen und es als seine Privatwohnung einzurichten, die nachts oft zu einem ungezwungenem Aufenthaltsort, zu einer Art Jazz-Bar wird, zu einem Treffpunkt mit seinen Freunden. In dem winzigen Zimmer seiner Tochter fällt die entzückende Tapete mit Herzmotiven auf und eine Wanduhr mit der beliebten Figur der „Hello Kitty".

Cette maison se trouve dans Kanda, la vieille ville de Tokyo, célèbre pour accueillir nombre de veilles librairies mais aussi le siège de maisons d'édition. Suite à l'héritage d'une imprimerie située dans le même immeuble, le propriétaire de cet appartement, autrefois musicien, décida de rénover le lieu selon son goût personnel. L'espace se transforme, de nuit, en un lieu informel de rencontre, de style bar de jazz, pour le propriétaire et ses amis. La petite chambre de sa fille affiche un délicieux papier peint aux motifs en cœur et une pendule suspendue avec le personnage de dessins animés « Hello Kitty ».

Esta casa se halla situada en el viejo barrio toquiota de Kanda, célebre por albergar un sinnúmero de librerías antiguas así como por ser sede de numerosas editoriales. Su propietario, después de heredar el negocio de imprenta familiar ubicado en el mismo edificio, decidió reformar este apartamento para convertirlo en su vivienda particular, la cual de noche suele transformarse en un espacio informal que, adoptando un cierto aire de bar de jazz, sirve como lugar de reunión para él y sus amigos. En la minúscula habitación de su hija destaca un precioso papel de pared con corazones como motivo de diseño y un reloj colgante con el personaje de historietas "Hello Kitty".

e-mail: flow_@mac.com Photos: Norikichi Completion date: 1999

This new house is located in a residential area in Tokyo's Suginami district. The head of this household is an ordinary white-collar worker, who shares the home with his wife and their school-age son. As the whole family is fond of music, they have placed their piano in a prominent position in the living room. Takanori Ihara, the young architect who designed this project, is a magnanimous professional who has made his name designing pleasant and comfortable living spaces. In the last few years he has not only been involved in building houses in Japan but has also been active abroad as well; for example, he has recently designed resort hotels in the Palau Islands, near the Philippines.

Dieses kürzlich erbaute Haus liegt in einer Wohngegend im Ortsviertel Suginami in Tokio. In dieser Wohnung leben der Familienvater, ein Büroangestellter, seine Ehefrau und ein Kind im Schulalter. Alle Familienmitglieder lieben Musik und stellten daher ihr Klavier an dem besten Platz im Wohnzimmer auf. Verantwortlich für die Durchführung dieses Projektes ist der junge Architekt Takanori Ihara, bekannt durch seine großzügigen Designs komfortabler Räumlichkeiten mit entspannender Atmosphäre. In letzter Zeit erregte er Aufmerksamkeit durch seine Hoteldesigns, die er in den Touristenbereichen des Archipels der Palau-Inseln in der Nähe der Philippinen durchführt.

Cette nouvelle maison habite la zone résidentielle de Suginami, un district de Tokyo. Le maître des lieux est un responsable administratif, habitant l'endroit avec son épouse et leur petit garçon. La famille étant mélomane, le piano s'est vu attribuer une place de choix dans le séjour. Takanori Ihara, le jeune architecte concepteur du projet, est un professionnel généreux et volontaire, connu pour créer des espaces plaisants et confortables. Récemment, non seulement s'est-il engagé dans le logement au Japon mais aussi à l'étranger, où il s'active dans la conception d'hôtels de villégiature dans les îles Palau, près de Philippines.

Esta casa, recientemente construida, está situada en una zona residencial del barrio de Suginami de Tokio. La vivienda está habitada por un padre de familia, empleado de oficina, su esposa y un hijo en edad escolar. Todos los miembros de esta familia son grandes aficionados a la música, así que optaron por colocar el piano en el mejor emplazamiento del salón comedor. El responsable de la realización de este proyecto es el joven arquitecto Takanori Ihara, un buen y noble profesional conocido por su diseño de espacios agradables y de ambientes relajados. Últimamente se distingue también por los proyectos de diseño de hoteles que está llevando a cabo en zonas turísticas del archipiélago de las islas Palau, cerca de Filipinas.

e-mail: flow_@mac.com Photos: Takeshi Taira Completion date: 2001

Photos: Yoshio Asakura Completion date: 1999

The building containing this flat is located in Daikanyama, a fashionable area in central Tokyo, well-known among young and middle-aged well-to-do urbanites for its restaurants, open-air cafes, fashion boutiques and furniture shops. This is a good example of a typical condominium inhabited by young professional couples. The main entrance is fitted with intercoms, video surveillance cameras, automatic postboxes big enough for parcels for all tenants, and an automatically mechanized three-story parking system. This 645-square foot flat boasts a living room, a main bedroom, under-floor central heating, air conditioning and a bathroom that can be converted into a drying room for clothes.

Das Gebäude dieses Apartments steht in Daikanyama, einem bekannten Statdteil im Zentrum von Tokio, der wegen seiner Restaurants, Straßencafés, seiner Boutiquen und Möbelgeschäfte besonders bei der Jugend der Hauptstadt sehr beliebt ist. Dieses Gebäude besteht aus Privatwohnungen, in denen junge Paare verschiedenster Berufe leben. Im Haupteingang der Immobilie sind Sprechanlagen, Sicherheitskameras, automatische Briefkästen für alle Bewohner installiert und außerdem gibt es ein automatisiertes, dreistöckiges Parksystem. Diese 60m² große Apartment umfasst ein Wohnzimmer, ein Hauptschlafzimmer, eine zentrale Fußbodenheizung, eine Toilette mit integrierter Warmwasservorrichtung, Klimaanlage und ein Badezimmer, das bei Bedarf in einen automatischen Wäschetrockner verwandelt werden kann.

L'immeuble accueillant cet appartement se situe à Daikanyama, un quartier à la mode du centre de Tokyo, bien connu des jeunes, et des moins jeunes, yuppies pour ses restaurants, cafés en terrasse, boutiques de mode et magasins de meuble. Cette construction est un bon exemple d'une résidence typique d'appartements privés habités par des jeunes couples de professionnels. L'entrée principale de l'édifice affiche interphones, caméras de vidéo-surveillance et boîtes à lettres automatiques pour chaque habitant, adaptées à la réception de paquets, et un système de garage mécanisé et automatisé, sur trois niveaux. L'appartement de 60 m² comprend un séjour, une chambre principale, un chauffage au sol, des toilettes avec coin lavabo intégré, l'air conditionné et une salle de bain convertible en buanderie pour sécher le linge.

El edificio en el que se halla este apartamento está situado en Daikanyama, una conocida zona del centro de Tokio, especialmente popular entre la juventud urbana de la capital por sus restaurantes, cafés al aire libre, y por sus tiendas de moda y muebles. El edificio está compuesto por pisos en régimen de propiedad horizontal y habitado por parejas jóvenes con profesiones liberales. La entrada principal al inmueble está equipada con interfonos, cámaras de seguridad, cajas automáticas para los inquilinos adaptadas para recibir paquetes y un sistema de parking automatizado de tres pisos. Este apartamento de 60 m² incluye un salón, un dormitorio principal, calefacción central ubicada en el suelo de parquet, aire acondicionado y un baño que se puede convertir en cuarto secador automático para la ropa.

The main characteristic of this building in the city of Chiba, exclusively given over to one-room apartments, is its attractive facade, covered with slatted aluminum shutters. This form of protection or concealment is reminiscent of traditional Japanese architectural devices like latticework (koshi) and reed screens (sudare). The use of louvred blinds on the building's facade gives its occupants the possibility of opening or closing them by hand from their balconies, thus creating a relationship between the residence and the outer street. As with the traditional "koshi" and "sudare", the choice of opening and closing the shutters to varying degrees allows the inhabitants of this building to modify the appearance of the facade.

Das Hauptmerkmal dieses Gebäudes in Chiba, das ausschließlich für kleine Studios mit einem Zimmer gebaut wurde, ist seine attraktive Fassade, die mit einer Art Rollläden aus Aluminiumlamellen verkleidet ist, die an die alten „Koshi"-Gitter und an die „Sudare" Rohrschirme der traditionellen japanischen Architektur erinnern. Die Mieter dieser Studios können nach Bedarf von ihren Balkonen aus die Lamellen der Rollläden öffnen oder schließen und schaffen so eine Beziehung zwischen Gebäude und Außenraum, während sie gleichzeitig das Bild der Fassade verändern.

Cet immeuble du centre de Chiba, accueillant exclusivement des logements d'une pièce, est principalement caractérisé par sa séduisante façade couverte de persiennes d'aluminium. Protection et camouflage, ces dernières ravivent pour l'observateur l'architecture japonaise traditionnelle, à base de « Koshi », treillis japonais, et de « Sudare », écrans de roseau. Les lames d'aluminium habillant l'immeuble offrent aux résidents des possibilités d'ouverture et de fermeture manuelles depuis leurs balcons, créant ainsi une relation optionnelle entre la résidence et la rue extérieure. Comme pour les « Koshi » et « Sudare » traditionnels, le choix d'ouvrir ou fermer les persiennes à des degrés variés permet aux habitants de l'édifice de modifier l'aspect de la façade.

La principal característica de este edificio, ubicado en la ciudad de Chiba y que acomoda exclusivamente pequeños apartamentos de una habitación, es su atractiva fachada, revestida de una especie de persianas de lamas de aluminio, que recuerda a los antiguos enrejados (koshi) y a las pantallas de caña (sudare) presentes en la arquitectura japonesa tradicional. Los inquilinos de estos pisos pueden opcionalmente desde sus balcones abrir o cerrar gradualmente estas persianas según sus preferencias, originando de este modo una relación entre el edificio y el espacio exterior. Los residentes del edificio modifican y modulan a su gusto la imagen de su fachada.

e-mail: spatial-design-studio@nifty.ne.jp Photos: Spatial Design Studio Completion date: 1998

Floor plan

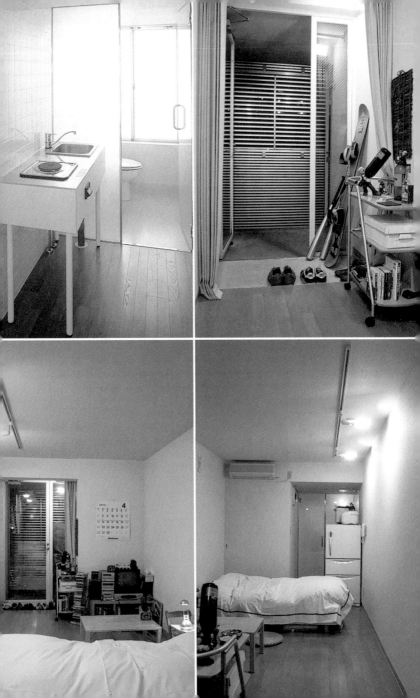

The condominium containing this apartment is located in Itabashi, near Ike-bukuro, an area well connected with central Tokyo by public transport. The building's architect intended the 645 square-foot flats –comprising a living/dining room and one bedroom– to provide pleasant, comfortable and secure accommodation for their tenants. The interior decoration of this particular apartment, featuring a number of objects and souvenirs picked up by the owner on her travels, contains a mixture of Japanese style and touches of other Asian cultures. As we can see from the large number of cookbooks and the extensive kitchen equipment, the owner, a graphic designer who lives on her own and works for a well-known weekly magazine, prizes good cooking.

Das Gebäude, in dem sich dieses Apartment befindet, steht in Itabashi in der Nähe von Ikebukuro, von wo aus man mit öffentlichen Verkehrsmitteln schnell ins Zentrum von Tokio gelangt. Die Architektin entwarf das Gebäude mit ca. 60m^2 großen Wohnungen mit Wohnzimmer und einem Schlafzimmer, die ihren Bewohnern einen freundlichen, komfortablen und sicheren Aufenthalt gewähren. Bei der Innendekoration dieses Apartments fallen Reiseandenken auf, die zusammen mit Gegenständen aus anderen Teilen Asiens durch die Vermischung des japanischen Stiles mit anderen ethnischen Eindrücken eine entspannende und ruhevolle Atmosphäre schaffen. Aus den vielen Kochbüchern und der vollendeten Küchenausstattung können wir schließen, dass die Bewohnerin, eine Graphikerin, die für eine bekannte Wochenzeitschrift arbeitet, Freude an gutem Essen hat.

La résidence hébergeant cet appartement se situe à Itabashi, près d'Ikebukuro, un quartier bien connecté par transport public au centre de Tokyo. Selon l'architecte, une femme, qui a conçu l'immeuble, chacun des appartements de 60 m^2 composé d'un séjour/salle à manger et d'une chambre offre un logement plaisant, confortable et sûr à ses occupants. La décoration intérieure de cet appartement, en particulier, comprenant nombre d'objets et de souvenirs de voyage collectés par le propriétaire, affiche un mélange de style japonais teinté par les goûts d'autres ethnies asiatiques. Comme nous le voyons de par le nombre de livres de cuisine et de plats, la propriétaire, une graphiste célibataire et travaillant pour un hebdomadaire célèbre, adore la bonne cuisine.

El edificio en el que se encuentra este apartamento está situado en Itabashi, cerca de Ikebukuro, una zona muy bien comunicada con el centro de Tokio. Según la arquitecta que diseñó el edificio, cada piso tiene unos 60 m^2, con un salón y un dormitorio, conformando un espacio agradable, confortable y seguro. En la decoración de este piso en cuestión destacan los objetos de recuerdos de viajes, mezclándose el estilo japonés con toques étnicos de otras partes de Asia, que infunden al mismo un ambiente relajante y pausado. Abundan también los libros de cocina y los platos decorativos. La inquilina del mismo es una diseñadora gráfica de un conocido semanario que disfruta de la buena comida.

Photos: **Seiko Baba** Completion date: **1997**

The Kitamura family home lies on the twelfth floor of a building situated in Tokyo's smart Aoyama district, famous for containing the main stores of famous fashion designers like Comme des Garçons or Yoji Yamamoto. The parents live happily together with their three daughters in this apartment measuring 1,000 square feet. The father, a devoted DIY fan, made, by hand, and later installed a whole shelf structure along one wall to house the audiovisual equipment. Being a typical Japanese consumer, he keeps on making additions to his work by adding new units as new products come onto the market. The window in the living room provides wonderful views of famous sights like the Tokyo tower.

Die Wohnung der Familie Kitamura liegt im 12. Stock eines Gebäudes des exklusiven Viertels von Aoyama, bekannt durch den Sitz der bedeutendsten japanischen Designer-Firmen wie z.B. Yoji Yamamoto oder Comme des Garçons. In dieser Wohnung von ca. 100 m² genießt ein Elternpaar mit seinen drei Kindern ein komfortables Leben. Der Vater, ein begeisterter Do-It-Yourself Fan, hat selbst die gesamten Regale gebaut und später mit allen audio-visuellen Geräten der Familie installiert. Als typischer japanischer Konsument von Neuerscheinungen passt er seine Anlage den jeweiligen Anforderungen an und verbessert sie gemäß den Platzerfordernissen. Vom Wohnzimmerfenster aus hat man eine klare Aussicht auf berühmte Gebäude der Stadt, wie z. B. auf den Turm von Tokio.

La demeure de la famille Kitamura se trouve au 12ème d'un immeuble situé dans Aoyama, le quartier élitiste de Tokyo, connu pour le nombre de magasins phares de créateurs célèbres, ainsi Comme de Garçons ou Yoji Yamamoto. Les parents habitent ensemble avec leurs trois filles dans ce logement de quelques 100 m². Le père de famille, fan de bricolage, a réalisé de ses mains puis installé sur le mur toute une structure d'étagères pour des produits audiovisuels. Consommateur japonais typique, le nombre de nouveaux produits augmentant, il continue de développer cette œuvre si particulière en lui ajoutant de nouvelles unités. Depuis la fenêtre du séjour sont observables des endroits célèbres comme la tour de Tokyo.

La casa de la familia Kitamura se encuentra en la planta 12 de un edificio situado en el exclusivo barrio de Aoyama, célebre por ser sede de las más importantes firmas del diseño japonés como Yoji Yamamoto o Comme des Garçons. Esta vivienda de unos 100 m² está ocupada por los padres y sus tres hijas. El padre, gran amante del bricolaje, ha construido e instalado todo el sistema de estanterías que contiene el equipo y productos audiovisuales de la familia. Como buen consumidor japonés de artículos novedosos, va adaptando y mejorando su particular obra en función de las necesidades de espacio requeridas. Desde la ventana del salón se ven perfectamente edificios célebres de la ciudad como la torre de Tokio.

Photos: Naruyasu Nabeshima Completion date: 1978

The company run by Takaharu and Yui Tezuka, who have, respectively, worked in Richard Rodger's studio in London and studied under Ron Herron in the University of London, is one of the most emblematic of young architectural Japanese firms. This house, situated in an uptown residential area of Kamarura called Kamakurayama, won an award from the Tokyo Society of Architects for successfully blending harmoniously into the hilly landscape and for creating a structure resistant to the humidity typical of Japan's climate. The interior of the house features large windows that seem to frame the outside scenery like paintings, and spacious rooms that provide great flexibility and an optimum ventilation.

Das Architektenbüro von Takaharu und Yui Tezuka wird von den jungen japanischen Architekten als das repräsentativste Büro im Land angesehen. Beide lebten in London, Takaharu arbeitete für Richard Rogers und Yui studierte unter der Leitung von Ron Herron an der Universität von London. Dieses Haus in der Oberstadt von Kamakura namens Kamakurayama erhielt den Preis des Architektenverbandes von Tokio, einmal wegen seiner erfolgreichen und harmonischen Verschmelzung mit der bergigen grünen Landschaft seiner Umgebung und zum zweiten wegen seiner widerstandsfähigen Struktur gegen die Feuchtigkeit des japanischen Klimas. Im Innenraum des Hauses umrahmen große Panoramafenster die Außenlandschaft. Die großzügigen Räume erlauben große Flexibilität und optimale Belüftung.

L'étude d'architecture de Takaharu et Yui Tezuka, ayant respectivement travaillé à l'atelier londonien de Richard Rogers et étudié sous l'influence de Ron Herron à l'université de Londres, est un des cabinets d'architecture les plus représentatifs parmi les jeunes architectes japonais. La maison, située dans une zone résidentielle chic de Kamakura nommée Kamakurayama, a remporté le prix de la Société des architectes de Tokyo pour se fondre harmonieusement avec le paysage vallonné environnant et pour sa structure adaptée à l'humidité inhérente au climat japonais. L'intérieur de la maison affiche de grandes fenêtres qui offrent une sorte d'encadrement au décor extérieur et des pièces spacieuses proposant flexibilité et ventilation optimum.

El taller de arquitectura de Takaharu y Yui Tezuka está considerado por los arquitectos jóvenes japoneses como uno de los más representativos del país. Ambos estuvieron residiendo en Londres, Takaharu trabajando para Richard Rogers y Yui estudiando bajo la dirección de Ron Herron en la Universidad de Londres. Esta casa, situada en la parte alta de una zona residencial de Kamakura denominada Kamakurayama, recibió el premio que concede la Asociación de Arquitectos de Tokio por conseguir una exitosa y armoniosa fusión con el montañoso y verde paisaje que la rodea, así como por su estructura, adecuada para prevenir la humedad del clima japonés. El interior de la casa tiene grandes ventanales que parecen enmarcar el paisaje exterior. Sus espaciosas estancias proporcionan gran flexibilidad y una óptima ventilación.

e-mail: **tez@sepia.ocn.ne.jp** Photos: **Katsuhisa Kida** Completion date: **1999**

Whereas the courtyards in European houses are enclosed by solid structures like walls so as to protect the inner space from the exterior, in Japan's traditional Machiya the courtyard is not concealed by any surrounding walls. Therefore, once the "Shoji" or the "Fusuma" have been opened, the cool breeze wind can pass through the whole house. This type of space provides a suitable means of combating Japan's harsh summer climate without any need to resort to air conditioning. This is an example of a contemporary Machiya house; although the architects have constructed a surrounding wall for reasons of privacy, the light and breeze can still flow right through the house.

Während die Innenhöfe der europäischen Häuser von soliden Wänden umgeben sind, um das Innen vor dem Außen zu schützen, sind die traditionellen japanischen Machiya offene Höfe ohne begrenzende Wände. Sobald also die „Shoji" oder die „Fusuma" geöffnet sind, kann die frische Brise des Windes das ganze Haus durchlaufen. Mit dieser wirksamen Methode kann man den harten klimatischen Bedingungen der Sommermonate in Japan begegnen und oft auf eine Klimaanlage verzichten. Dieses moderne Beispiel des Hauses Machiya zeigt, wie Licht und Luftzug das Haus durchströmen, obwohl die Architekten das Haus zum Schutz der privaten Atmosphäre ihrer Bewohner umzäunt haben.

Alors que les cours des maisons sont, en Europe, enveloppées par des structures solides comme des murs, afin de protéger l'espace intérieur de l'extérieur, dans le Machiya japonais traditionnel, elles ne sont occultées par aucune cloison environnante. De ce fait, dès que le « Shoji » ou le « Fusuma » sont ouverts, une brise fraîche peut s'insinuer dans toute la maison et dans les suivantes. Sans nécessiter d'air conditionné, ce type d'espace offre un moyen adapté pour combattre le dur climat de l'été japonais. Il s'agit donc d'un exemple contemporain de la maison Machiya qui, bien que les architectes l'aient entourée d'une barrière pour protéger la vie privée, laisse affluer air et lumière au cœur de la maison.

Mientras que los patios interiores de las casas en Europa están rodeados de sólidas estructuras en forma de pared para proteger los interiores del exterior, en el caso de las tradicionales machiya japonesas, los patios son espacios abiertos sin paredes a su alrededor. Así, al correr los "Shoji" o "Fusuma", el espacio resultante permite la entrada y el paso de aire fresco por toda la casa. Este método es altamente eficaz para combatir el duro clima japonés durante el verano a la vez que permite prescindir en muchos casos de la instalación de aire acondicionado. En este ejemplo contemporáneo de casa machiya, a pesar de que los arquitectos han erigido una valla alrededor del edificio para mantener la intimidad de sus inquilinos, la luz y la corriente de aire continúan entrando en la casa.

e-mail: tez@sepia.ocn.ne.jp Photos: Katsuhisa Kida Completion date: 2000

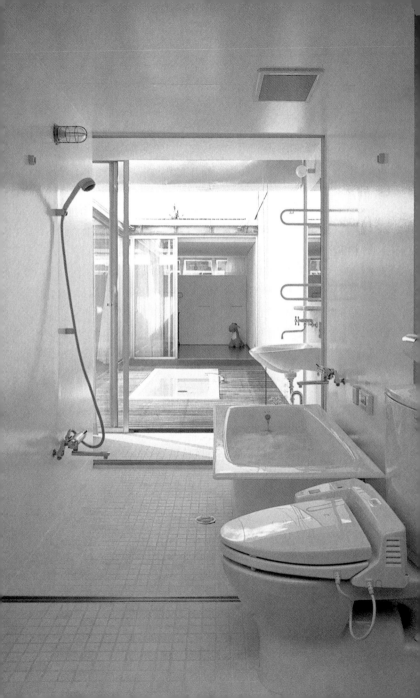

Tezuka's architectural office has designed not only a host of comfortable and pleasant living spaces but it has also brought to life some highly imaginative one-off projects: a new type of hospital, a condominium for young Japanese musicians with impeccably soundproofed walls, etc. This house is located in Kamakura, near Enoshima and Tokyo's conurbation. Overlooking the Pacific Ocean, its structure bears a slight resemblance to a megaphone. Among other distinctive features, it is worth mentioning the facade's exterior curtains, looking like the sails of a boat, and the huge window measuring 30 x 20 feet, which frames the lanscape outside as if it were a painting. It is such an inviting space that its occupants can seldom be persuaded to leave it when they have days off work.

Abgesehen davon, dass das Architekten-Büro Tezuka viele komfortable und entspannende Projekte verwirklicht hat, ist es auch bekannt durch die Planung von Projekten wie z. B. eine neue Art von Krankenhaus, ein mehrstöckiges Gebäude für junge Musiker mit perfekter Wandisolierung, etc. Dieses Haus steht in Kamakura in der Nähe von Enoshima und Tokio. Mit Aussicht auf den Pazifischen Ozean erinnert sein Anblick an ein Megaphon. Unter anderen Besonderheiten sind die Außengardinen der Fassade zu erwähnen, die Schiffssegeln gleichen sowie das große Fenster von 9m x 6m, das den Horizont wie ein Gemälde einrahmt. Dieser Ort ist so entspannend und einladend, dass seine Bewohner ihn nur selten an Feiertagen verlassen.

L'étude d'architecture Tezuka a conçu nombre d'espaces plaisants et confortables, mais également donné corps aux rêves de ses clients en projetant des travaux comme un nouvel hôpital, une résidence pour de jeunes musiciens japonais dotée de cloisons parfaitement insonorisées, etc. Cette maison est située à Kamakura, près d'Enoshima et de la conurbation de Tokyo. Surplombant le Pacifique, la structure a une légère ressemblance avec un mégaphone. Parmi ses caractéristiques singulières, il convient de mentionner les rideaux extérieurs de la façade, telles les voiles d'un bateau, et la vaste baie vitrée de 9 x 6 m, enveloppant l'horizon comme en un encadrement. Ce lieu est un espace séduisant d'où ses habitants s'échappent rarement en fin de semaine et pour les vacances.

El estudio de arquitectos Tezuka, aparte de diseñar un buen número de espacios agradables y relajantes, también es conocido por haber dado rienda suelta a proyectos de clientes como un nuevo tipo de hospital o un edificio de pisos para músicos jóvenes con una impecable insonorización en las paredes. Esta casa se halla en Kamakura, cerca de Enoshima y de la conurbación de Tokio. Con vistas al océano Pacífico, su estructura recuerda ligeramente a la de un megáfono. Entre otras peculiaridades, cabría destacar las cortinas exteriores de la fachada, con aspecto de vela de barco, y el gran ventanal de 9 m x 6 m que enmarca la línea del horizonte como un cuadro. Este es un espacio relajante y agradable del que sus habitantes apenas salen durante los días de fiesta.

e-mail: tez@sepia.ocn.ne.jp Photos: Katsuhisa Kida Completion date: 2000

This house was drawn up to satisfy the needs of a three-generation household. One member of the third generation, an architect, designed it in conjunction with some of his colleagues. On top of the parking lot there is a terrace that curves slightly upwards so as to prevent passing cars and pedestrians in the street from being able to see inside the living room. The architects paid particular attention to even the smallest details in the living space on the first floor given over to the grandparents, to make sure that they did not feel isolated. So, they have the possibility of being able to take showers in a wheelchair and feeding the fish in the courtyard below from their own private room.

Dieses Haus wurde gebaut, um die Bedürfnisse eines 3-Generationen-Haushaltes zufrieden zu stellen. Einer der Architekten, selbst ein Enkel des Hauses, entwarf zusammen mit seinen Mitarbeitern das Gebäude für seine Familie. Über dem Parkplatz befindet sich die leicht nach oben geneigte Terrasse, um das Wohnzimmer vor den Blicken Vorbeigehender und Autos zu schützen. Das erste Stockwerk wird von den Großeltern bewohnt und dort haben die Architekten ihre ganze Phantasie spielen lassen und an die kleinsten Details gedacht, um größte Bequemlichkeit zu bieten, angefangen mit der Möglichkeit, im Rollstuhl zu duschen, bis hin zur Fütterung der Fische im kleinen Teich des Außenhofes vom eigenen Zimmer aus.

Cette maison a été pensée pour répondre aux attentes d'un foyer de 3 générations. L'un des architectes, petit-fils au sein de la famille, a conçu avec d'autres collègues cette demeure pour sa famille. Une terrasse, au-dessus du garage, se courbe légèrement vers le haut pour éviter que passants et voitures ne puissent jeter un œil depuis la rue dans le séjour. Quant à l'espace de vie des grands-parents au premier, les architectes ont pensé à chaque détail afin d'éviter leur sensation d'isolement : de la capacité de se doucher en chaise roulante à la possibilité de nourrir les poissons dans la cour depuis leur propre chambre.

Esta casa fue proyectada para satisfacer las necesidades de una familia compuesta por tres generaciones. Uno de los nietos forma parte del estudio de arquitectos que diseñó el edificio para toda su familia. En la parte superior del parking se encuentra la terraza, con una ligera inclinación ascendente para evitar u obstruir en cierta medida las miradas de la gente y coches del exterior dirigidas hacia el salón. En cuanto al espacio del primer piso destinado a los abuelos, los arquitectos dieron rienda suelta a su imaginación, pensando hasta el más ínfimo detalle para proporcionarles la máxima comodidad, desde la posibilidad de tomar duchas en silla de ruedas hasta poder alimentar desde su propia habitación a los peces del pequeño estanque situado en el patio exterior.

e-mail: t-hosaka@yhb.att.ne.jp Photos: Kozo Takayama (Façade) & New House Co.Ltd.
Completion date: 2000

Approximately 25 miles from the center of Tokyo lies Hayama, a beautiful area not far from the old capital city of Kamakura blessed with scenic views of Mount Fuji and the Pacific Ocean. This area also contains one of the summer palaces belonging to the Imperial family as well as a good number of marina yacht harbours. This house, situated on the seafront, revels in the many seasonal changes in scenery on Mount Fuji and in the ocean. It was designed by Speed Studio, an architectural office based in the Kanagawa district and made up of young architects who are still in their twenties. This studio had already won acclaim with their Nishida 3-Generation House.

Etwa 40 km von Tokio entfernt liegt Hayama, eine bezaubernde Gegend in der Nähe der alten Hauptstadt Kamakura mit herrlicher und spektakulärer Aussicht auf den Berg Fuji und den Pazifischen Ozean. In der Nachbarschaft liegt einer der Sommerpaläste der kaiserlichen Familie sowie zahlreiche Sporthäfen mit Segelbooten. Die Bewohner dieses Hauses am Meer können hier ebenso die je nach Jahreszeit wechselnde und vielfältige Landschaft des Fuji und des Pazifischen Ozeans genießen. Speed Studio, ein Architektenbüro in der Präfektur von Kanagawa, dessen Mitarbeiter alle jünger als dreißig Jahre sind, entwarf dieses Gebäude. Das Studio war bereits bekannt geworden mit dem Entwurf des 3 – Generationen – Hauses Nishida.

Hayama se situe à une quarantaine de kilomètres du centre de Tokio. Elle se trouve à proximitè de l'ancienne capitale Kamakura et jouit d'une vue spectaculaire sur le Fuji-Yama et l'ocean pacifique. De nombreux ports de plaisance ainsi que l'une des résidence d'été de la famille royale se trouvent également dans les alentours. Cette maison, située face à la mer, jouit d'un encadrement et d'un paysage très varié et changeant selon les saisons sur le Fuji-Yama et le Pacifique. Le Speed Studio, un bureau de jeunes architectes dans la trentaine en conçût le design. Cette équipe s'étant déjà fait un nom antérieurement avec leur projet Nishida: la Maison 3 Générations.

A unos 40 kilómetros del centro de Tokio se halla Hayama, una bonita zona cerca de la antigua capital Kamakura, dotada asimismo de preciosas y espectaculares vistas sobre del monte Fuji y el océano Pacífico. Cerca se encuentra también uno de los palacios de verano de la familia imperial, así como numerosos puertos deportivos de navegación a vela. En esta casa, situada frente al mar, sus habitantes pueden disfrutar también del variado paisaje, cambiante en función de la estación, del monte Fuji y del Pacífico. Speed Studio, un taller de arquitectura cuyos jóvenes componentes no sobrepasan aún el umbral de los treinta años y ubicado en la prefectura de Kanagawa, diseñó este edificio. Anteriormente el estudio había ganado ya renombre con el proyecto de la Nishida 3 Generation House.

e-mail: t-hosaka@yhb.att.ne.jp Photos: Shinkenchiku-sha Completion date: 2001

Tezuka architectural office is accustomed to turning their clients' most whimsical dreams into reality. This is its motto. In this case, they realized a family's dream of spending most of the day on top of the roof of their house, located in Tokyo's Hachioji area. The roof contains 8 skylights, one for each member of the family plus a special one situated in the bathroom, so that the occupants can observe the sky from the bathtub. The roof can be reached through any of the 8 skylights by simply leaning a ladder against it. In Japan it is customary to eat "somen" (cold pasta) outdoors in the summer. Nevertheless, this family's way of observing this custom is somewhat original.

Die Parole des Architekten-Büros Tezuka ist die Verwirklichung der meisten und manchmal sehr extravaganten Träume ihrer Kunden. Der Traum der Familie in diesem Haus im Viertel von Hachioji in Tokio, die meiste Zeit auf dem Dach ihres Heimes zu verbringen, wurde so in die Praxis umgesetzt. Hier wurden 8 Dachfenster angebracht, eines für jedes Familienmitglied, sowie ein weiteres im Badezimmer, um während des Bades die Sterne beobachten zu können. Der Zugang zum Dach geht über eine Leiter, die an jedes der Dachfenster angelehnt werden kann. In Japan isst man während der heissen Sommermonate im Freien „Somen" (kalte Nudeln). Die Familie pflegt diese Sitte auf recht originelle Art.

L'étude d'architecture Tezuka a l'habitude de transformer en réalité les rêves fantasques de ses clients. C'est l'axiome de Tezuka. Pour cette demeure du quartier tokyoïte de Hachioji, le rêve de la famille, passer la plupart de leur journée sur le toit de leur maison, a donc été mis en pratique. 8 claires-voies ont été insérées dans la ligne de toiture, une pour chaque membre de la famille, plus une additionnelle pour la salle de bain afin que, tout en se baignant, chacun puisse contempler le ciel. Le toit est accessible par une échelle, reposable contre chacune des claires-voies. En été, au Japon, il est de coutume de déguster du « somen » (nouilles froides) à l'extérieur. Cette famille a, pour autant, une façon bien à elle de respecter la coutume.

El lema del taller de arquitectura Tezuka es poder hacer realidad la mayoría de los sueños de sus clientes, por disparatados que parezcan. Así, realizaron el particular sueño de esta familia, cuya casa está en el barrio de Hachioji de Tokio, y que se reducía, ni más ni menos, a poder hacer vida encima del tejado. Éste contiene ocho ventanas tragaluz, una para cada miembro de la familia, además de una especialmente situada en lo alto de la sala de baño para que sus moradores puedan gozar de la visión de las estrellas mientras toman un baño. El acceso al mismo se lleva a cabo mediante una escalera a través de cualquiera de los tragaluces. En Japón, es costumbre comer pasta fría (somen) al aire libre durante el caluroso verano, hábito que esta familia cumple de forma muy original.

e-mail: tez@sepia.ocn.ne.jp Photos: Katsuhisa Kida Completion date: 2001

The Maru Gallery, which specializes in contemporary Japanese art, is located in a dramatic airy loft looking directly onto Tokyo Bay. The space encompasses both an exhibition area and private living quarters. The Maru Gallery director Kara Besher, a native of Manhattan, has been living in Tokyo since 1985, where she has organized exhibitions and symposiums as well as writing on Japan's art market and contemporary art. The 19-foot-high gallery windows offer Besher outstanding views of the constant changes in the landscape in areas like Odaiba and Shinagawa, where large architectural projects always seem to be in progress.

Die Maru Galerie für moderne japanische Kunst befindet sich in einem weiträumigen, luftigen und aufsehenerregenden Loft mit Blick auf die Bucht von Tokio. Ein Teil der Räumlichkeiten wird für Ausstellungen genützt, ein anderer Teil für Privatwohnungen. Kara Besher, die Leiterin der „Maru Gallery", in Manhattan (N.Y.), geboren, wohnt seit 1985 in Tokio. Besher organisiert nicht nur Ausstellungen und Symposien, sondern schreibt auch über moderne Kunst und über den Kunsthandel in Japan. Von den über 5 Meter hohen Fenstern der Galerie betrachtet Besher als privilegierte Zuschauerin die konstanten Wechsel des Stadtbildes von Tokio.

La galerie Maru, spécialisée en art contemporain japonais, se situe dans un superbe loft spacieux, face à la baie de Tokyo. L'espace accueille une zone d'exposition et un lieu de vie. La directrice de la galerie Maru, Kara Besher, native de Manhattan (N.Y.), vit à Tokyo depuis 1985. Elle organise depuis lors expositions et symposiums tout en écrivant sur le marché de l'art et l'art contemporain japonais. Besher, depuis les baies de 5,4 m de haut de sa galerie, est une observatrice privilégiée de l'évolution constante du paysage du nouveau Tokyo, contemplant des quartiers tels Odaiba et Shinagawa, sites de nouveaux et vastes projets architecturaux incessants.

La galería Maru, especializada en arte contemporáneo japonés, se halla en un espacioso, aireado y espectacular loft que da a la bahía de Tokio. El espacio incluye tanto un área para realizar exposiciones como también dependencias utilizadas como vivienda particular. Kara Besher, directora de la galería y natural de Manhattan (Nueva York), reside en Tokio desde 1985. Besher, además de organizar exposiciones y simposios, escribe sobre arte contemporáneo y sobre el mercado del arte en Japón. Desde los ventanales de la galería, de más de 5,4 metros de altura, Besher es una observadora privilegiada de los cambios constantes del paisaje urbano de Tokio.

e-mail: arts@tki.att.ne.jp Photos: Naruyasu Nabeshima Completion date: 1997

Andrea Held & Akira Hikone http://members.aol.com/aha004/aha.html

Eri Nakada http://www17.u-page.so-net.ne.jp/bd5/nakada1/

flow architecture http://homepage.mac.com/flow_/

Guen Bertheau-Suzuki http://users.arcmedia.co.jp/gbs

Katushi Nagumo http://www.nagumo-design.com/

Kara Besher http://www.marugallery.com

Love the Life http://www.lovethelife.org

Mikan http://www.mikan.co.jp/

milligram Studio http://www.milligram.ne.jp

Mori Building Co. Ltd. http://www.mori.co.jp/residence

Nobuaki Furuya / Studio Nasca http:// www.studio-nasca.com/

Spatial Design Studio http:// homepage2.nifty.com/sds/menu.html

Takaharu and Yui Tezuka Architects http://www.tezuka-arch.com

Takashi Iwama http://www.socius.co.jp

Takatsuka Architects Firm http:// www.takatsuka-architects.com

Tatsuo Iwaoka http://bosei.cc.u-tokai.ac.jp/~iwaoka/

Yukio Hashimoto http://www.din.or.jp/~hydesign.

Other Designpocket titles by teNeues:

Berlin Apartments 3-8238-5596-4

Cafés & Restaurants 3-8238-5478-X

Cool Hotels 3-8238-5556-5

Country Hotels 3-8238-5574-3

Exhibition Design 3-8238-5548-4

Furniture/Möbel/Meubles/Mobile Design 3-8238-5575-1

Italian Interior Design 3-8238-5495-X

London Apartments 3-8238-5558-1

Los Angeles Houses 3-8238-5594-8

New York Apartments 3-8238-5557-3

Office Design 3-8238-5578-6

Paris Apartments 3-8238-5571-9

Product Design 3-8238-5597-2

Showrooms 3-8238-5496-8

Spa & Wellness Hotels 3-8238-5595-6

Staircases 3-8238-5572-7

Each volume:

12.5 x 18.5 cm
400 pages
c. 400 color illustrations